UTILITY REGULATION:
CHALLENGE AND RESPONSE
The State of Britain's Regulatory Régime

Graeme Odgers • Ian Byatt
Alan Bell • Clare Spottiswoode
John Swift QC • Rt. Hon. Christopher Chataway
Professor Stephen Littlechild • Sir Bryan Carsberg

Discussed by
Thomas Sharpe QC • Dieter Helm • Professor John Kay
Professor Geoffrey Whittington • Ian Jones
Professor Rigas Doganis • Professor Colin Robinson
Sir Christopher Foster

Introduced and edited by
Professor M.E. Beesley

**Institute of Economic Affairs
in association with the
London Business School
1995**

First published in June 1995

by

THE INSTITUTE OF ECONOMIC AFFAIRS
2 Lord North Street, Westminster, London, SW1P 3LB

in association with the
London Business School

IEA Readings 42
All rights reserved

ISSN 0305-814X

ISBN 0-255 36349-4

Cover design by David Lucas

Printed in Great Britain by
Bourne Press, Bournemouth, Dorset

Text set in Times Roman 11 on 12 point

UTILITY REGULATION:
CHALLENGE AND RESPONSE

CONTENTS

INTRODUCTION

Professor Michael E. Beesley
London Business School

1994 WAS A VINTAGE YEAR for students of UK regulation, arguably one in which its attributes were most thoroughly displayed. It was duly reflected in this, the fourth LBS Regulation Lectures series, held in the Autumn of 1994 and the third to be organised jointly with the IEA. In two of the large utilities, water and electricity, the respective regulators had the opportunity to make major price reviews, and in doing so, had their first chance substantially to modify the decisions on prices (alongside much else) handed them by the Government on privatisation.

In gas, following the 1993 MMC report and the Secretary of State's subsequent decisions on the gas references, the Regulator had the task of creating and making work a new structure for British Gas. This was intended, in effect, to reverse the main mistake made on privatisation, namely, the failure clearly to separate the natural monopoly from the competitive activities. In telecoms, the Government's decisions following the 1990 Duopoly review, to free competitive entry, but without structural change in the incumbent BT, came home to roost in enhanced agonising about the proper way to charge for interconnect and to shape and monitor BT's accounts. In rail, the Regulator started the formidable task of devising key determinants of commercial relationships in an as yet unachieved privatisation.

Moreover, these searching tasks had to be carried out against a background of increasingly critical attention from all the stakeholders in regulation – consumers, politicians and, not least, the regulated companies themselves. Hence the emergence of some of the themes taken up in the lecture series. Perhaps the most significant of the criticisms has been the questioning of regulatory processes: How far should the specialist regulator be made more subject to appeal mechanisms? Should the reliance on a single regulator be modified, and if so, in what new forms? A possible interpretation of the upsurge of criticism is that the specialist regulators' increasingly effective confrontation of the privatised incumbents has generated understandable responses not only from the incumbents, but also from those particular consumer interests which, before privatisation, had been the beneficiaries of nationalised industries' pricing behaviour.

The lectures and discussions recorded in this volume of *IEA Readings* reflect the regulators' different positions in the development of the privatisation process, which certainly did not stop with the passage of the Acts or with the flotations. In many ways, the specialist regulators were (and are) engaged in the continuing task of defining the 'natural monopoly' elements of their respective industries, so defining the actually or potentially competitive – a task itself changing over time in response to technological developments in supply, proceeding everywhere but most clearly manifest in telecoms. The logical counterpart of increasing competitive scope is retreat by specialist regulators from regulating competition on their patches, leaving the field to the generalists, OFT and MMC. But this logic presupposes a competent pro-competitive – or at least anti-monopoly – framework. That the specialists have such prominent pro-competitive duties – and all have been concerned to use these as vigorously as their Act allows – is evidence of a weak UK law on abuse of a dominant market position. As will be seen, the issue of making the general competitive arrangements in the UK more effective is tackled by several of the contributors and in contrasting ways.

This is indeed a main theme taken up by **Christopher Chataway** in his paper on air charter regulation, and by his discussant, **Rigas Doganis**. Both are concerned about combating the power of large airlines. Christopher Chataway argues from the vantage point of a specialist regulator whose office pre-dates privatisation and covers a wide range of air industry activities. His paper and Rigas Doganis's comments will also be of particular interest to readers because of their expositions of a regulator's long-term strategy in forwarding competition. In these contributions, the practice of the art of the possible in regulatory affairs is vividly demonstrated.

Meanwhile, and perhaps paradoxically, for one of the generalist regulators, the MMC, 1994 was a relatively quiet year. The MMC is the principal means for incumbents to appeal utility price control decisions but in the end it was used for only one of the 14 electricity decisions (Scottish Hydro) and two of the 38 water decisions (Portsmouth and South West), perhaps less than the MMC itself had expected. Opinions about this relative lack of protest against regulators in practice have varied, from deeming the regulators to have been too soft to the view that a just balance of interests had been achieved. Both have their reflection in the papers that follow: *first*, by **Dieter Helm** in appraising water and (by comparison) more strongly in criticising electricity decisions; and *second*, in the expositions of **Ian Byatt** and **Stephen Littlechild**, which reject the criticisms by implication. Dieter Helm thinks that the shortcomings in procedures and decisions will generate a political reaction which will markedly increase ministerial influence on the regulators.

While appeals to the MMC are proceeding, neither regulator could reply to critics. **Ian Byatt** gives a thorough review of the procedures leading up to his pricing decisions, a complex and lengthy process of definition of issues and discussion by interested parties. This is, I believe, the most comprehensive such review yet to appear. **Sir Christopher Foster**, later in the series, describes it as 'painstaking and careful'; it was, doubtless, helped by the relatively uncomplicated technical and economic issues water faces ('relatively', that is, to those in rail and electricity; water has many of its own complications). Stephen Littlechild in his lecture looks forward to future regulatory needs in electricity, in particular to the further development of effective competition and to improving information for controlling the actual monopoly elements in electricity. His contribution was notable, participants thought, for its new policy content, as in his reference to the need to reconsider separation of RECs' activities. For **Colin Robinson**, commenting on Stephen Littlechild, what the Regulator can do, given the hand he has to play, is clearly not sufficient. He emphasises the need, as he sees it, to correct the original mistakes of privatisation in electricity by creating more players in generation, including privatising separate nuclear companies.

In 1994, **Clare Spottiswoode** received some help in her task of creating new competitive structures and rules in gas. After a considerable period of doubt about the political will to use a Parliamentary legislative slot, the Queen's speech (delivered just after her lecture) announced that the legislation required to remove obstacles embodied in the 1986 Privatisation Act, which did not anticipate major modification of British Gas's market dominance, would be enacted in this Session. As her paper indicates, this clears the way to adopt an agenda for change not otherwise possible. For **Geoffrey Whittington**, since the legislation will not provide for British Gas's divestiture, as recommended by the MMC, there is clearly a chance that reform will not be sufficient. But he recognises the need to make 'the best of a bad job', and is cautiously hopeful about competition. The Gas Regulator is indeed in an exceptional position among regulators in having some initiative in proposing legislation. This is a perhaps unanticipated consequence of the Secretary of State's decision to reject the MMC's 'great remedy', as Geoffrey Whittington terms it, but nevertheless to promote competition in gas; to do so he gave the Regulator considerable freedom to decide issues affecting company structure, in line with much of MMC's argument.

Regulatory cognoscenti may well find that the ratio of information per 100 words of text is highest in **John Swift's** paper, not least because, of all regulatory situations, that in rail has been the most obscure. Amongst other things, rail is unique in having a dual regulatory structure: the task of generating competition is given to the Franchise Director, Mr Roger Salmon, while the Regulator, John Swift, sets competitive terms. Of particular interest, therefore, is John Swift's explanation of his relationship with the Franchise Director. This is especially so because while the Regulator has the formal independence from Government common to the other regulators, the Franchise Director is a Department of Transport official, as befits one who is responsible for the very large subsidy required to run railways.

Ian Jones, in his comment, is very sceptical about whether the present privatisation scheme in rail, involving franchising, is viable at all. He argues that the basic model will have to be revamped, in effect because the hoped-for numbers of franchisees will not be forthcoming under the present scheme. A common underlying theme of both the rail contributions is the impact which the decision to privatise Rail Track early in the privatisation timetable will have on the Treasury's original ambitions to reduce subsidy through imposing a target of an 8 per cent return on Rail Track's assets, assessed by using the 'modern equivalent asset' method of valuation.

For Oftel, like Ofgas, 1994 was a year of intensive negotiation with the incumbent about the future terms on which its networks would be used by rivals. **Alan Bell** gives a view, from mid-engagement, on the central issue of interconnect, to be revisited, perhaps fundamentally, for the first time since the most important regulatory decision of the 1980s, the interconnect agreement of 1985, was made. **John Kay** thinks that the debate in this area is in many ways outdated and creates non-existent problems. He looks to recent theoretical developments in economics, and in accounting practice, to resolve the 'cost allocation problem' others have found so difficult to handle.

UK regulation as a whole is, we are told, influential in the lessons it gives to the rest of the world in reforming regulation. Interconnect is an issue in which international trade in ideas is clearly reciprocal, since other administrations have had to face the same critical decision. It is certain that the economic contributions to the current debate, initiated by Alan Bell's paper and the Consultation Document which followed hard on its heels, will apply overseas lessons (for example, from Australian and New Zealand experience); the latter indeed culminated in a Privy Council ruling handed down during the lecture series.

Specialist regulators (and the generalists before them) were established to be remote from direct Ministerial intervention. This does not absolve them from Ministerial influence; and 1994 was a time of very active interchange between Ministers and specialist regulators, as the papers show. By contrast, for the MMC and the OFT, the year was one of rather little ministerial activity. **Graeme Odgers** reviews the MMC's functions and character in his rebuttal of the criticism implied in the title of his paper; he argues that its apparent weaknesses – as in its lack of powers to initiate and follow up cases – are its strengths. He wishes to preserve, rather than to find new rôles for, the MMC, but cautiously endorses the idea that the MMC should be involved when actions of the specialist regulators may imply major structural or competitive change in their industries. **Tom Sharpe** is, however, unsparing in his criticism not only of MMC's competences and procedures but also, by implication, of the Government's inaction – its failure to follow up its promises to reform competition law, still pigeonholed after four years. (Many of his points about the need for remedies for abuse of monopoly power recall those I made in this series last year.)[1] He clearly thinks that either the UK law will be reformed, or will increasingly be by-passed by substitute legal actions in the UK or Europe.

Bryan Carsberg, in what proved to be one of his last public lectures before announcing his resignation from the post of Director General of Fair Trading, leaves us with quite far-reaching suggestions for change in the law in this area, in particular to adopt *per se* prohibitions not only in restrictive practices (a long-standing suggestion) but also in certain abuses of monopoly power. Predatory pricing and, in particular, refusal to supply are his examples. The contrast between Tom Sharpe's and Bryan Carsberg's reform agendas will, no doubt, greatly interest the reader.

Christopher Foster's main worry returns to the question of ministerial-regulatory relationships. The spotlight has recently been on regulators' due process, perhaps too critically; he thinks it should also be turned on politicians. He argues that Ministers' decisions on policy affecting industries, and their particular decisions affecting competition in all regulators' affairs, should be more clearly stated and rationalised, and so open to appraisal.

This volume will, I believe, prove an interesting record of the state of play in UK regulation at a most testing time. No doubt many of the problems thrown up here will be developed in the Autumn of 1995, when academics are to give the lectures in the fifth Regulation Series, chaired by the Regulators who will lead the subsequent discussion.

London Business School **M.E.B.**

April 1995

---

[1] M.E. Beesley, 'Abuse of Monopoly Power', Chapter 8 in M.E. Beesley (ed.), *Regulating Utilities: The Way Forward*, IEA Readings No.41, London: Institute of Economic Affairs in association with the London Business School, 1994, pp.139-60.

THE AUTHORS

Michael Beesley is a founding Professor of Economics, now Emeritus, at the London Business School. Lecturer in Commerce at the University of Birmingham, then Reader in Economics at the LSE, he became the Department of Transport's Chief Economist for a spell in the 1960s. His recent work has centred on the issues of deregulation and privatisation in telecoms, transport, water and electricity, and he is currently Economic Adviser to OFGAS and OFFER. He started the Small Business Unit at the School, a focus for entrepreneurship.

His independent economic study of *Liberalisation of the Use of British Telecommunications' Network* was published in April 1981 by HMSO and he has since been active as an adviser to the Government in telecoms, the deregulation of buses and the privatisation of the water industry. For the IEA, of which he is a Managing Trustee, he wrote (with Bruce Laidlaw) *The Future of Telecommunications* (Research Monograph 42, 1989) and (with S.C. Littlechild) 'The Regulation of Privatised Monopolies in the United Kingdom', in *Regulators and the Market* (IEA Readings No.35, 1991). He has edited all three of the previous volumes in this lecture series, the third of which, *Regulating Utilities: The Way Forward*, was published as IEA Readings No.41 by the IEA in association with the LBS in 1994.

He was appointed CBE in the Birthday Honours List, 1985; and he became Director of the PhD programme in the same year. In 1988 he became a member of the Monopolies and Mergers Commission.

Alan Bell has been Director of Economics at the Office of Telecommunications (OFTEL) for the last five years. He has been involved with many of the major issues OFTEL has addressed, including the 1991 Duopoly Review, the setting of price controls in 1992, accounting separation for BT, and interconnection issues, including the BT/Mercury determination in 1993.

He has worked as a government economist since 1973. Before moving to OFTEL he was involved in technology assessment in the Cabinet Office, appraisal of industry support schemes and advice on IT industries at the DTI, and advice on monopolies and mergers at the Office of Fair Trading.

Ian Byatt was appointed as the first Director General of Water Services on 1 August 1989. He is an economist and an expert on the regulation of public utilities. His previous post was as Deputy Chief Economic Adviser to the

Treasury (1978-89). He was born in 1932 and educated at Kirkham Grammar School and at St Edmund Hall and Nuffield College, Oxford. He also studied at Harvard University as a Commonwealth Fund Fellow. He has lectured in economics at both Durham University (1958-62) and the London School of Economics (1964-67).

He joined the Civil Service in 1967 as Senior Economic Adviser to the Department of Education and Science. His career in the Civil Service also included spells at the Ministry of Housing and Local Government and the Department of Environment, before joining the Treasury in 1972. In 1986 he chaired the Advisory Committee on Accounting for Economic Costs and Changing Prices.

His publications include *The British Electrical Industry 1875-1914* (1979).

Sir Bryan Carsberg has been Director General of the Office of Fair Trading (OFT) since June 1992. He was previously Director General of the Office of Telecommunications (OFTEL) from 1984 to June 1992. He qualified as a Chartered Accountant in 1960. After four years in private practice, he became a lecturer in accounting at the London School of Economics and Political Science (LSE) and a visiting lecturer at the University of Chicago. He gained an MSc (Econ.) at the London School of Economics in 1967. In 1969 he was appointed Professor of Accounting and Head of the Department of Accounting and Business Finance, University of Manchester, and later Dean of its Faculty of Economic and Social Studies. From 1978 to 1981 he was Assistant Director of Research and Technical Activities and Academic Fellow with the Financial Accounting Standards Boards, USA. In 1981 he became Arthur Andersen Professor of Accounting at the LSE and part-time Director of Research for the ICA. He is the author of numerous accountancy publications and has also undertaken various consultancy assignments in accounting and financial economics. For the IEA he contributed a paper, 'Competition and the Duopoly Review', to *Regulators and the Market* (IEA Readings No.35, 1991). He was awarded his knighthood in January 1989.

The Rt. Hon. Christopher Chataway's career has been divided between the public and private sectors. After reading PPE at Magdalen College, Oxford, and four years with ITN and the BBC, he was a Member of Parliament for North Lewisham (1959-66) and Chichester (1969-74). He was a junior Education Minister in the Macmillan Government (1962-64) and Minister in the Heath Administration (Minister of Posts and Telecommunications, 1970-72; Minister for Industrial Development, DTI, 1972-74; appointed PC in 1970). From 1974 he was for 15 years Managing Director of Orion Royal Bank. He has been a non-executive Chairman or Director of a number of companies since 1974. He became Chairman of the Civil Aviation Authority in June 1991.

Rigas Doganis is Head of the Department of Air Transport in the College of Aeronautics at Cranfield University. He has carried out consultancy work for many airlines, airports, and government and international agencies in the UK, Europe and the Far East, and has been an adviser to the House of Commons Select Committee on the Nationalised Industries and the House of Lords Select Committee on the European Communities.

His numerous papers on airline and airport economics and management include *Flying Off Course: The Economics of International Airlines* (first published in 1985 with a substantially enlarged second edition in 1991); and *The Airport Business* (October 1992). He is founder editor of *The Journal of Air Transport Management*, a Fellow of the Royal Aeronautical Society and the Chartered Institute of Transport.

Sir Christopher Foster has had a career in academia, government and business. He has been adviser to the Chairman of Coopers & Lybrand since 1994. He was previously senior public sector and economics partner of Coopers & Lybrand Associates. He is a non-executive director of Railtrack, the RAC and the LDDC. He advised on the privatisation of BAA, BT, PowerGen and, on rail privatisation, as special adviser to the Secretary of State for Transport from 1992-94. He has written a book on regulation, *Privatisation, Public Ownership and the Regulation of Natural Monopoly* (Blackwells, 1992), and several subsequent papers, mostly published as pamphlets by the Centre for Regulated Industries. He has been a Fellow of Jesus College, Oxford (1958-66), and a full-time then visiting Professor of Economics at the LSE (1971-85).

Dieter Helm is a director of Oxford Economic Research Associates Ltd. and a Fellow in Economics at New College, Oxford. His previous appointments include Research Fellow in Economics and Management, New College, Oxford, 1981-83, Lecturer in Economics, Queen's College, Oxford, 1983-86, Senior Research Fellow, Centre for Business Strategy, London Business School, 1987-88. He is a Research Associate of the Institute for Fiscal Studies, and was the founding Managing Editor (now an Associate Editor) of the *Oxford Review of Economic Policy*. He is Editor of *Energy Utilities*.

Ian Jones is a director of National Economic Research Associates' London office, where he heads their transport practice and is a senior member of the competition policy team. He has been extensively involved in debates on railway privatisation as an adviser to the Department of Transport, as well as to British

Rail and Railtrack. The opinions expressed in his contribution to this *Readings* are his own.

John Kay is Visiting Professor of Economics at the London Business School, and co-founder of London Economics. He was previously Research Director of the Institute for Fiscal Studies, and Fellow of St John's College, Oxford. He is the author or editor of several books, including (with Mervyn King) *British Taxation System* (1978); (with Jeremy Edwards and Colin Mayer) *The Economic Analysis of Accounting Profitability* (1987); and (with Colin Mayer and David Thompson) (eds.) *Privatisation and Regulation – The UK Experience* (1986). For the IEA he contributed 'The Forms of Regulation', in *Financial Regulation – or Over-Regulation?* (IEA Readings No.27, 1988).

Stephen Littlechild was appointed the first Director General of Electricity Supply on 1 September 1989. He has been Professor of Commerce, University of Birmingham, since 1975. He was formerly Professor of Applied Economics, University of Aston, 1973-75, and sometime Consultant to the Ministry of Transport, Treasury, World Bank, Electricity Council, American Telephone & Telegraph Co., and Department of Energy.

He is author or co-author of *Operational Research for Managers* (1977), *Elements of Telecommunication Economics* (1979), and *Energy Strategies for the UK* (1982). For the IEA he wrote *The Fallacy of the Mixed Economy* (Hobart Paper 80, 1978, Second edn. 1986), and contributed to *The Taming of Government* (IEA Readings 21, 1979) and *Agenda for Social Democracy* (Hobart Paperback 15, 1983). He has been a Member of the IEA Advisory Council since 1982. He was commissioned by the Department of Industry to consider proposals to regulate the profitability of British Telecom. His reports, *Regulation of British Telecommunications' Profitability*, and *Economic Regulation of Privatised Water Authorities*, were published in 1983 and 1986.

Graeme Odgers was appointed Chairman of the Monopolies and Mergers Commission (MMC) in April 1993, having been a part-time member of the Commission from the previous January. He was born and educated in South Africa, read engineering at the University of Cambridge and gained an MBA at Harvard Graduate School of Business Administration in 1959. He worked for a period with the International Finance Corporation in Washington, DC, and settled in England in 1962. His varied career has embraced both the public and private sectors. He was Head of the Industrial Development Unit at the DTI in the mid-1970s, Finance Director and then Managing Director of Tarmac PLC, Managing Director of BT, and Chief Executive of Alfred McAlpine PLC.

Colin Robinson was educated at the University of Manchester, and then worked for 11 years as a business economist before being appointed to the chair of Economics at the University of Surrey in 1968. He has been a member of the Electricity Supply Research Council and of the Secretary of State for Energy's Advisory Council for Research and Development in Fuel and Power (ACORD), and is currently on the electricity panel of the Monopolies and Mergers Commission. He has written widely on energy and regulation. His most recent IEA papers are *Making a Market in Energy* (IEA Current Controversies No. 3, December 1992), and *Energy Policy: Errors, Illusions and Market Realities* (IEA Occasional Paper No.90, October 1993).

Professor Robinson became a member of the IEA's Advisory Council in 1982 and was appointed its Editorial Director in 1992. He was appointed a Trustee of the Wincott Foundation in 1993. He received the British Institute of Energy Economists' award as 'Economist of the Year 1992'.

Thomas Sharpe, QC, was educated at Trinity Hall, Cambridge, and, with degrees in Economics and Law, was called to the Bar in 1973. He held part-time appointments as an adviser to the Secretary of State for Trade and Industry on aspects of telecommunications, liberalism and competition, 1981-83; Executive Director, Institute for Fiscal Studies, 1981-87; special consultant, NERA, 1984-88; 'Of Counsel' Gibson Dunn & Crutcher, London and Los Angeles, 1984-88. He entered practice at the Bar in 1987 and was appointed a QC in 1994. He has been involved in many MMC inquiries, has advised extensively in all aspects of EC competition law, and also various Hong Kong telecommunications regulatory problems.

He has contributed widely to legal journals and is a frequent lecturer on competition and regulatory topics. He is a member of COMBAR, Bar European Group and the British Institute for International and Comparative Law.

Clare Spottiswoode was appointed Director General of Gas Supply (OFGAS) on 1 November 1993, for a term of five years. She graduated in mathematics and economics at the University of Cambridge in 1975, and was awarded a Mellon Fellowship to Yale University where she took a further degree in economics. She began her career as an economist with the Treasury in 1977, leaving in 1980 to start a family and found a business which traded in gifts. Having sold it as a going concern, she started a software company specialising in microcomputer software packages for the financial and corporate sector. She sold this company in 1988, remaining as Managing Director and Chairman until 1990.

Since then she has increased her family whilst holding several part-time appointments, including being a tutor at the London Business School's Centre for Enterprise and a member of the Government's engineering deregulation task force.

John Swift, QC, was appointed Rail Regulator and International Rail Regulator (Office of the Rail Regulator) in December 1993, having previously been special adviser on the railway privatisation regulatory framework to the Secretary of State for Transport from January to November 1993.

He was born in 1940 and educated at Birkenhead School and University College, Oxford, where he gained MA with first-class honours in the School of Jurisprudence in 1963. He then gained a Diploma with Distinction at the Johns Hopkins School of Advanced International Studies at Bologna, 1963-64. He became a Barrister at Law in 1965, a QC in 1981, and a Barrister of the Inner Temple in 1992.

Geoffrey Whittington is Price Waterhouse Professor of Financial Accounting at the University of Cambridge and a Professorial Fellow of Fitzwilliam College, and a member of the Monopolies and Mergers Commission. He is Academic Adviser to the Accounting Standards Board. He is a Chartered Accountant and also holds a doctorate in Economics. He has previously served as a member of the Technical and Research Committees of the Institute of Chartered Accountants in England and Wales, and as a part-time economic adviser to the Office of Fair Trading.

1

MMC: TALKING SHOP OR DECISION-MAKER?

Graeme Odgers
Monopolies and Mergers Commission

A LEADING COMMENTATOR ON UK COMPETITION LAW has described it as a 'bizarre and complex structure'.[1] How right he is! We in the MMC work under eight separate statutes ranging from the Fair Trading Act through the Competition Act, the various privatised industry acts, to the Broadcasting Act. And we are only one of a number of institutions concerned with regulating competition.

The current legal framework has developed gradually into this complex structure over the last 50 years. The various privatisations in the 1980s multiplied the complexities. There are further changes in progress under the Deregulation and Contracting Out Act 1994 and yet further changes promised when Parliament finds time to address restrictive trade practices and market dominance. Our regulatory system, like all others, has strengths and weaknesses – but it is not well understood.

I shall discuss how the MMC operates within this complex system, dealing with it in two parts: first, what I might call the traditional private sector (leaving out the privatised utilities) and, secondly, the privatised utilities themselves. The underlying principles apply broadly across both sectors; the mechanics of course vary. The question I want finally to focus on is: 'Is The MMC talking shop or decision-maker?' Or putting it in other words: 'The MMC – is it a powerful body, is it an influential body, or is it a waste of time and money?'

The Private Sector

Starting with the MMC and the private sector, let us briefly review the background of the UK system and the principal players in it.

Modern competition regulation in the UK was established by legislation

---

[1] R. Whish, *Competition Law*, Third Edition, London: Butterworths, 1993, p.730.

in 1948 via the Monopolies and Restrictive Practices Act. It was based on the philosophy, *first*, that authorities should not intervene in normal commercial behaviour unless and until it was determined that a particular situation was operating or was expected to operate *against the public interest*. And, *second*, that the judgement about the public interest should only be made following a thorough and even-handed investigation by an independent body.

This basic philosophy still lies at the heart of our system. In dealing with monopolies, mergers and anti-competitive practices a set of checks and balances are in place as well as a separation of functions which are designed to ensure maximum fairness of investigation and objectivity of judgement. The separation of the functions is between what I might loosely call 'prosecution', 'judiciary' and 'executive'.

Starting with *'prosecution'*, we have the Director General of Fair Trading (DGFT), Sir Bryan Carsberg, in charge of the Office of Fair Trading. The OFT receives complaints, makes preliminary investigations and tries to sort out problems. The DGFT can be seen as a watchdog concerned with monitoring the interests of customers, with anti-competitive behaviour by companies and/or industries, and with mergers. If he becomes particularly concerned about a situation and feels it merits a full inquiry or if he cannot sort it out through appropriate action or undertakings, he can refer to the MMC. In monopoly cases or anti-competitive practice cases, he refers direct to the MMC. In merger cases he makes recommendations to the Secretary of State about whether or not a reference should be made.

The second function, *the 'judiciary'*, falls to the MMC. We receive our references from the DGFT or from the Secretary of State. We *cannot* instigate our own references. Our inquiries must be thorough and even-handed. Our judgements are about the public interest. All our reports are published and must indicate clearly how we reached our conclusions. We are independent of government. We are independent of the OFT. If we judge a matter *not* to be against the public interest our judgement stands as final. This happened recently, for instance, with fine perfumes, with recorded music and with ice-cream freezers.[2] Our judgements there were the end of the matter. You might say that therein lies our power. If, on the

---

[2] *Fine fragrances: A report on the supply in the UK for retail sale of fine fragrances,* Cm. 2380, London: HMSO, November 1993; *The supply of recorded music: A report on the supply in the UK of pre-recorded compact discs, vinyl discs and tapes containing music,* Cm. 2599, HMSO, June 1994; *Ice cream: A report on the supply in the UK of ice cream for immediate consumption,* Cm. 2524, HMSO, March 1994.

other hand, we decide the matter *is* against the public interest, we make *recommendations* for change. These recommendations are just that, and it is for the executive to decide what, if any, final action should be taken. Recent examples of adverse findings are contact lens solutions, newspaper distribution and private medical services.[3] The third function is the *'executive'*. This falls to the Secretary of State for Trade and Industry. The Secretary of State is required by statute to take fully into account our report and our recommendations. Herein you might say lies our influence. But he may, after appropriate consideration, decide differently from the MMC. He may decide to take no action at all or he may decide not to follow a particular recommendation. Mr Neil Hamilton,[4] acting for the Secretary of State, did this recently in the case of newspaper distribution where we had recommended a limited remedy related to the sub-retailing of newspapers. Mr Hamilton decided to go further than this and, in consultation with the industry, developed a detailed code of practice governing the supply of national newspapers to retail outlets.

There may be occasions from time to time where I might feel personally disappointed that the Secretary of State does not follow our recommendations. But in law and in practice I and the MMC have no standing in the matter after the MMC has delivered its report. Our function ends there. This is part of the system of checks and balances. I actually believe that it is right that if substantive changes are required of an industry, it should be the Government, responsible to Parliament, that makes the final decision. Its rôle after all is to govern.

How the MMC Operates

I have said that we are a body independent of government – in reaching our decisions we are *not* subject to governmental policy of the day or to political expediency. However, the members of the MMC are *appointed* by the Government. There is only one full-time member, namely myself, the Chairman. I am on a four-year contract. There are three Deputy Chairmen on three-year renewable contracts who work 3^1/2 days a week on MMC matters. Then there are some further 30 members who can work up to an average of 1^1/2 days a week as required. These members are

---

3 *Contact lens solutions: A report on the supply within the United Kingdom of contact lens solutions,* Cm. 2242, London: HMSO, May 1993; *The supply of national newspapers: A report on the supply of national newspapers in England and Wales,* Cm. 2422, HMSO, December 1993; *Private medical services: A report on agreements and practices relating to charges for the supply of private medical services by NHS consultants,* Cm. 2452, February 1994.

4 Mr Hamilton was then the Parliamentary Under Secretary of State for Corporate Affairs at the DTI.

3

appointed for three years, usually renewed for a further three years. They come from a great variety of backgrounds – business, finance, the professions, academia and the trade unions. We have five women members and I would like to see that number increase. Many members are well known in their particular fields. The fact that we draw on them *part-time* allows us to have access to a depth of experience that would not be available to us if members were required to be employed full-time.

When a new reference comes in I, the Chairman, decide which members will handle the inquiry. I normally appoint a group of four or five members under the chairmanship of myself or one of my Deputy Chairmen. While clearly I need to know what is going on in each inquiry, under the Fair Trading Act it is the *group* that makes the MMC judgement. I as Commission Chairman cannot overrule the group's judgement. There is discussion and consultation between group Chairmen and myself about the major issues and I sit in from time to time on group meetings. I always do this in a way which preserves the autonomy of the group.

The group is supported on an inquiry by a team of MMC staff. We currently have a total staff of about 80 under the general management of our Commission Secretary. The staff includes economists, accountants, lawyers, industrial advisers and administrators. Much of the basic work on individual inquiries is done by the staff team led by a team leader. We are currently considering how we can best make use of outside consultants on inquiries.

Our inquiries, as I have said, must be thorough and they must be even-handed. By their nature they are burdensome to the main parties involved. Substantial questionnaires must be answered and intensive hearings attended. Great importance is attached by the parties to their submissions and to the hearings because large, commercial interests are often at stake.

As I explained earlier, our judgements are about the *public interest*. The Commission is required under the Fair Trading Act to take into account *all* matters which appear to it in the particular circumstances to be relevant. And, among other things, it must have regard to the desirability:

- of maintaining and promoting effective competition in the United Kingdom;

- of promoting the interests of consumers in respect of prices, quality and the variety of goods and services supplied;

- of promoting efficiency and innovation and facilitating the entry of new competitors into existing markets;

- of promoting the balanced distribution of industry and employment in the United Kingdom; and

- of promoting the international competitiveness of United Kingdom industry.

The range of considerations against which we determine the public interest is very broad. In theory it could lead to arbitrary or inconsistent judgements across inquiries. In practice I believe this does not happen because of the form of collegiate management we adopt in the MMC. I meet fortnightly with my Deputy Chairmen and the Commission Secretary to discuss all matters relating to the MMC and, in particular, the on-going inquiries. Remember that between myself and my Deputy Chairmen we cover the chairmanship of practically all individual inquiry groups. We analyse the inquiries at key stages of development – that is, at the start, when main issues are identified, and when conclusions are being reached. Thus, we are able to feed into and feed off each other. We refer back to previous MMC reports where lessons can be drawn. We aim to ensure consistency of procedure as well as of economic analysis. We seek a sensible pragmatism of approach which takes into account the particular circumstances of each situation. But, as mentioned earlier, ultimately the decision on any individual inquiry is for the *group* dealing with it.

On each inquiry a balance has to be struck between many factors, many interests, often in conflict with each other. Because of this our findings are often controversial. There can be winners and losers. Often there are substantial commercial consequences related to our findings. The winners tend to walk away contentedly, but quietly. The losers feeling oppressed by our judgements, may vent their discontent loudly.

Some commentators (and this particularly applies to certain consumer groups) take the view that our public interest criteria should be dominated by consumer interests – in particular, prices. We have been accused of neglecting the consumer interest and 'selling out' to industrial interests. This is not the case. In every inquiry we take fully into account the consumer interest – we are, after all, obliged to do so under the Act.

At the heart of our inquiries is the test of competition. If a market is competitive and likely to remain so, we are unlikely to find against the public interest. If, on the other hand, competition or potential competition is weak and dominance, coupled with the abuse of dominance, takes place – whether this is in relation to competitors, to suppliers or to customers – we are likely to find against. In assessing competition we look at many facets – prices, concentration in the industry, barriers to entry, scope for substitution, bargaining power of buyers and sellers, strength of international competitors, profitability, and so on.

In my view there is no contradiction between this approach of focusing on competition, and the concept of promoting the interests of consumers. A competitive environment over the medium and the longer term is the one most likely to serve the interests of consumers in terms of prices, quality and range of goods and services.

Does the System Work?

Before moving on to the privatised utilities I will summarise the strengths of the present system.

- The basic principles have stood the test of time over nearly 50 years. Over the decades those principles have proved appropriate despite the enormous changes in the economy that have taken place.

- It allows for intervention only when the situation is acting against the public interest. The principle 'if it ain't broke don't fix it' applies. It allows a company which has built up legitimate competitive advantage through innovation, investment, entrepreneurship and efficiency to exploit that advantage up to the point where the company dominates a market and then starts to abuse its market position. Thus it encourages those factors that generate a vibrant, dynamic, free enterprise economy.

- The judgements are made by an independent body made up of high calibre members from a wide range of backgrounds. The judgements are unaffected by prosecutory zeal or by political factors.

- The reports of the MMC, being full and published, help ensure the transparency of the process.

- Finally, the system recognises the right of government to govern in that, when an adverse public interest finding is made, the MMC recommendations are just that, recommendations, with the final decision on major changes being left in the hands of government.

The Privatised Utilities

Turning now to the regulation of the privatised utilities, I will consider the background to the regulatory structure and the specific role of the MMC. The privatisation of the major public utilities began in 1984 with

British Telecommunications (BT). Since then the process has been extended to include airports, gas, water and electricity, with railways to follow. The privatised utilities are now a very important part of the total economy. Broadly speaking, on privatisation the utilities moved from being public monopolies to being private monopolies, retaining their ability to dominate their particular fields of activity. It followed, therefore, that some form of special regulation of their activities was required. Since then, competition has, to varying degrees, emerged.

The privatisation Acts each deal with the process of privatisation and the provision of specific industry regulation through a regulator. The regulation is additional to existing UK competition law. The various regulatory regimes have many points in common, but they also have major differences. Generally speaking, regulators are required to promote competition, protect customers and promote various social objectives such as the provision of services for the old and disabled. Regulators normally operate through the vehicle of licences granted initially by the Government to the privatised company.

A regulator can propose amendments to a regulated company's licence, which may include changes in pricing. If the company agrees, the amendment will be implemented. If, however, agreement cannot be reached, and if the regulator wishes to proceed with the amendment, he will refer the matter to the MMC.

When a reference is made, the MMC is required to decide whether any of the matters referred operate, or may be expected to operate, against the public interest. In determining the public interest the MMC does not apply the criteria of the Fair Trading Act but rather the specific criteria set out in the relevant privatisation Act. This may, for instance, include the ability of the company to *finance* the provision of the relevant services.

If an adverse finding is made the MMC's recommendations *must* be taken into account by the regulator but, having done so, it is generally up to him to make the final decision on the licence amendment. An exception to this is a price control reference in relation to a water company where the decision of the MMC is binding.

I should also note that under the Water Industry Act, the Secretary of State is required to make a reference where water companies over a certain minimum size are to merge. Such references are governed by the public interest criteria of the Fair Trading Act, together with the desirability of maintaining the ability to make comparisons of performance by water companies across the UK.

The Airports Act also differs from the other Acts in that it *requires* the Civil Aviation Authority (CAA) to make references to the MMC every

7

five years regarding airport charges. The MMC's recommendations are *not* binding on the CAA.

In addition to the particular powers to make references which I have described, most industry regulators have powers concurrently with the DGFT to make monopoly references for their industries under the Fair Trading Act and anti-competitive practice references under the Competition Act.

References to Date

The MMC has to date received relatively few references in respect of the privatised utilities – fewer, I believe, than had been expected when the legislation governing the sector was introduced. Whether this is a result of the strengths or weaknesses of the system is for debate.[5]

References have been made under the Telecommunications, Gas, Water and Airports Acts. In the case of telecommunications, we were asked to look into the narrow areas of chatline and message services over the BT network. In the case of gas, we have received references under the Fair Trading Act from the DGFT in 1987 and from the Secretary of State in 1992. We had simultaneous references under the Gas Act from the industry regulator in 1992. In each of these references, the MMC made adverse findings and proposed a number of wide-ranging remedies. We have had three water industry merger references and have reported three times on airport charges.

The Future

The regulatory system governing the privatised utilities has been the subject of much comment and a degree of criticism. It has been suggested, for example, that:

- the system has placed too much power in the hands of individual regulators who are not sufficiently accountable for their actions;

- there is no requirement on the regulators to ensure transparency in their dealings with regulated companies – for example, they are not required to give reasons for their decisions;

- there is a risk, within the system, of regulatory capture which could lead to a regulator paying insufficient attention to the interests of consumers;

---

5 Since the lecture we have received two price control references under the Water Industry Act and one reference under the Electricity Act.

- the system allows the regulators to come to arrangements with regulated companies involving major structural and competitive change within the industry without such major policy matters being properly considered by the Government, and indeed Parliament.

I do not propose to comment on each of these criticisms. But I would like to address a number of suggestions for changes in the role of the MMC which have arisen out of them.

First, it is suggested that the MMC should become involved at a much earlier stage and in a limited way, to sort out relatively narrow disputes between regulator and regulatee. A 'mini MMC reference' is called for. This, it is claimed, would curb the excessive power of the regulator by giving the regulated company easier and earlier access to an independent arbiter.

Second, it is suggested that where the regulator is considering questions of major structural or competitive change within an industry, this should come to the MMC under a Fair Trading Act reference. This would ensure that a thorough, independent, disinterested investigation is undertaken and a report published, with the final decision on these important policy matters being made by the Government should an adverse public interest finding be made by the MMC.

Finally, it is suggested that where it appears to a responsible body (say an industry users' committee or appropriate parliamentary committee) that there may have been regulatory capture, these bodies should approach the DGFT. If after investigation the DGFT has major concerns about the situation, he could propose to the Secretary of State that a monopoly reference be made to the MMC under the Fair Trading Act.

Dealing with the first of these suggestions, the 'mini MMC reference', this appeals to me not at all. We, the MMC, would soon become the effective industry regulator on most contentious matters and the appointed regulator's role would be seriously undermined.

The second suggestion, that the MMC should get involved in cases where major structural or competitive change within an industry is on the cards, sounds to me to be both sensible and consistent with the basic philosophy of the UK's competition regulatory system.

The third suggestion on regulatory capture also has some merit but would need careful handling to avoid frivolous references demanded by groups driven by populist as opposed to true consumer interest motives.

All these suggestions for MMC involvement are possible under existing legislation. It is up to the referring powers to judge when such matters should be referred. As I have already made clear, the MMC can take no initiative in instigating its own references.

The MMC – Talking Shop or Decision-Maker?

Let us finally turn to the question: The MMC – is it a talking shop or a decision-maker? Is it a powerful body, an influential body, or is it a waste of time and money?

The MMC has power in that it is the final decision-maker on references where we come to no adverse public interest findings. Where we come to adverse public interest findings, we make recommendations. These *must* be taken into account by the regulator or Secretary of State, and in this sense we are influential. But with one or two notable exceptions, the final decision lies not with us but with the executive.

The mere fact that the MMC exists also has an important influence, outside the field of individual references. Powerful companies know that if, on their own or with others, they come to dominate their industries and they then abuse that dominance, they are likely sooner or later to face the MMC. If they are found to be acting against the public interest they may find this to be a distinctly uncomfortable experience. They will, therefore, hesitate to behave in anti-competitive ways.

As for the regulators, they will be careful in handling their affairs to come to sensible agreements with the regulatees. A regulator will wish to ensure that, in any reference to the MMC, the exposure that this entails will enhance his or her standing in the eyes of the industry and the public, rather than the reverse.

Is the MMC a talking shop? Certainly a great deal of discussion takes place at our offices in Carey Street. But after one and a half years in the Chairman's seat I am broadly content that our UK regulatory system works pretty well and that the MMC's own rôle of carrying out thorough, even-handed and transparent investigations is a valuable one.

DISCUSSANT'S COMMENTS

Thomas Sharpe QC

IT IS VERY DIFFICULT TO TAKE too much exception to such a reasonable presentation as the one Graeme Odgers has given. Although I was billed speculatively as being controversial, because I have a healthy regard for the Monopolies and Mergers Commission, I want to communicate that regard at the outset, perhaps to balance what I am about to say.

Nor will I join the claque which criticises reports on the grounds that prices have not been reduced by 50 per cent, or the price of this or that is higher in England than it is in New York! I think that sort of criticism does no credit to anyone: practically everything is more expensive in England than in New York. As a starting point it might be of use; as a conclusion, it is irrational.

There is a mismatch between public expectation as articulated in newspapers, and especially through the Consumer's Association under its present management, and the reality of the position of those who are faced with an inquiry by the Monopolies Commission and those who do the inquiries, the Commission itself. The mismatch is unhealthy. Perhaps it is due to the difficulties associated with understanding what the Commission's rôle is. The Chairman has most effectively defined it in his paper.

The MMC: 'A Great Survivor'

MMC is one of the great survivor institutions. Very few public institutions of the 1940s are still up and running. All the public corporations, or most of them, the Planning Boards, the marketing organisations, National Board for Prices and Incomes, Price Commission, NEDO and all the others, have been decently interred over the last 40-odd years, leaving what was, at its inception, the Monopolies and Restrictive Practices Commission. It has not merely survived, it has prospered and expanded. It has acquired new rôles and responsibilities. Monopolies in goods were insufficient to keep it engaged and, as we have heard, it was extended to services, the privatised utilities, utility licences, the press, anti-competitive practices,

11

broadcasting and airports. The White Paper on Opening Markets[1] in 1989, which if not buried is certainly, shall we say, laid out, would give it responsibility for cartels and exemptions of various agreements as well. It is now a large organisation: 35 commissioners, 80 staff and, as Graeme Odgers's paper indicated (above, p.4), private consultants are to be brought in to manage inquiries.

It is perhaps worth reflecting at the outset why it lost jurisdiction over cartels in 1956. The Commission was held in low regard in the mid-1950s. This supports one of the Chairman's remarks: there has never been a time when the Monopolies Commission has been popular. Industry was dissatisfied with its performance, lack of clarity and predictability and opted for a system in which there would be judicial certainty, combined with lay assessors, clearly defined notions of what was an agreement and what the restriction was, and the obligation to register, that is, a legal solution. In 1968 the remedies of damages and injunctions for giving effect to registrable agreements which have not been registered were added.

The alternative, started in 1948 and carried on under the Monopolies Commission after 1956, is quite different. It is administrative, as we have heard, practical and pragmatic. To call this 'competition law' is, I have always thought, something of a vanity to which lawyers all too readily succumb. It is not really law in the sense of providing rules, guidance for future action, remedies and compensation. The only rôle that law plays is to provide a framework within which public powers can be exercised. I will discuss in a moment the virtual absence of effective judicial review of the Monopolies Commission's decisions and its processes.

To repeat, the Commission has never been popular and some reform or other is always in the offing. Those of us who have laboured in the vineyards of the Public Records Office will see that in 1963 the failure of our entry into the European Community prompted Harold Macmillan to realise the British economy was thoroughly uncompetitive and to think that the Monopolies Commission was failing the nation. He thought it ought to do more to ginger up industry now that French and German competition would no longer be able to do so as a result of our non-membership of the Community. The Government of the day was susceptible to the criticism they were doing nothing. To dispel that impression it immediately referred household detergents, soap powders and colour films to the Monopolies Commission, recalling that at the time references were political measures. According to the record, this was pretty well the only reason why these industries were referred.

---

[1] *Opening Markets: New Policy on Restrictive Trade Practices*, Cm. 727, London: HMSO, 1989.

And then came the Leisner 1 and Leisner 2 reviews;[2] the legislative change of the Competition Act 1980; and the 1992 Green Paper,[3] which is (I was going to say) dead but was at least sidelined in April 1993. But an official responsible for the Act in 1948, returning to this meeting, would find the model pretty well intact. The Commission is essentially a mini Royal Commission on each subject of inquiry.

The MMC's Reference Procedure

I want to isolate four or five aspects of the procedure. *First*, the Monopolies Commission has no jurisdiction to initiate its own inquiries. Matters must be referred to it by the OFT, or for mergers, the Secretary of State, or if it is a utility matter, the Regulator.

In many cases this accounts for the oddity of some of the references and perhaps more importantly for the oddity of timing. The most vivid example was referring the motor industry to the Commission during the worst recession anybody in the motor industry can remember. The industry was regarded as a complex monopoly; its members were regarded as having the power to prevent, restrict or distort competition. To accuse members of that particular industry at that time of having market power just when most had seen their sales collapse to roughly 50 per cent of what they had been one or two years earlier, was mind-bogglingly bad timing. Even if the reference was appropriate, irrespective of timing, what remedies would have been appropriate in a time of such deep recession?

The suggestion is occasionally made that the division between the Office of Fair Trading and the Monopolies and Mergers Commission has served its purpose and that the two bodies ought to be brought together. What was termed the prosecutorial or investigatory aspect of the process should be merged with what was termed the adjudication aspect of the process.

This idea ought not to be rejected out of hand. If I recall correctly, it was adopted and approved by the House of Commons Select Committee on Trade and Industry. It certainly has its attractions. I doubt very much if the independence of the Commission would be lost; I do not regard the Office of Fair Trading as anything other than an independent body. It may add some robustness, being an enlarged body with greater responsibilities.

It might be accompanied by a greater full-time component of the Commission. That is not to say that the part-time element need go

---

2 *A Review of Monopolies and Mergers Policy*, Cmnd. 7198, London: HMSO, 1978; *A Review of Restrictive Trade Practices Policy*, Cmnd. 7512, HMSO, 1979.

3 *Abuse of Market Power*, Cm. 2100, London: HMSO, 1992.

completely; there is much force in the argument that good people may not wish to make a career change to serve on a public body, and there is equal force in the argument that a public body ought to have access to people with wide and continuing experience. But all of us involved in this know that it can sometimes be extremely difficult to bring together a panel of five individuals, all of whom by definition are busy, all of whom have something to contribute to other spheres and for whom the Monopolies Commission is not the centre of their universe. They have obligations to their shareholders, their partnerships or whatever. And I refuse to believe that a spell of full-time activity on the Monopolies Commission would not, for some people, be a valuable career move, and a very attractive position to be in.

Amalgamate the OFT and the MMC

Equally, the amalgamation of the two institutions, the OFT and the Monopolies Commission, would bring together two sources of skilled and experienced staff. I am afraid I cannot subscribe to the view that we are oversupplied with good industrial economists, good officials versed in competition and the range of knowledge that requires. To divide them three ways between the OFT, MMC and DTI seems to me to be spreading available resources rather thinly. At the very least, bringing the two institutions together would eliminate the overlap of staff and concentrate competence and information. For other reasons, to be further explained later, I think OFT and the Commission should come together.

The *second* aspect is that an inquiry is, above all, an administrative process. To me, the most important manifestation of this is that the DTI defines what is to be investigated. In order to investigate anything, there must be a monopoly of 25 per cent of a relevant market. In every other competition jurisdiction I know of – that is, the European Community, the United States, Australia, New Zealand and Canada – there is a major threshold argument as to what the relevant market is. This is the key to understanding whether or not an undertaking has market power; or, to put it another way, whether the investigation is going to be worthwhile.

In those jurisdictions, the inquiry about the relevant market is a complicated, lengthy, sophisticated investigation, typically into the availability of substitutes. If the relevant market is such that there are substitutes, there is likely to be no market power. If so, in my view, the authorities would have to consider long and hard whether there was any particular issue to be debated. It could be the end of the story.

The position is very different for the Monopolies Commission. The definition of the market is an administrative matter now decided by the

Office of Fair Trading, no doubt after a good deal of consideration, but never as much as it deserves, and certainly without public consultation, and with nothing like as much debate as you would find elsewhere in the EC and America. The final judgement is an administrative one, and once made is not one that is capable of being debated as a question of jurisdiction before the Monopolies Commission.

Now obviously in an inquiry, any adviser worth his salt is going to say to a client, 'we must try and define the relevant markets, because our percentage is negligible', with the inference that there is no market power. But there is no formal point in the inquiry where that is done. Instead, it is a matter for the OFT.

If it were a threshold question, some investigations would have ended then and there. It would have been said that the particular products in question were so substitutable that it was ridiculous for that undertaking to be subject to a lengthy and expensive inquiry when it plainly faced competition.

But, in practice, as the Chairman said, the early stages of an inquiry are essentially wading through a paper mountain. I recall one bank merger a couple of years ago, when in the last three days of what proved to be a two-week reference, no less than 24 inches of documents landed on my desk. Many of those questions were thoroughly irrelevant to the threshold question I have posed which in that, and most references, is the only question worth asking.

Fair Trading Act Criticised

The Fair Trading Act as an Act is looking very ragged. It has been subjected to a number of unsuccessful challenges as to what is meant by a 'complex monopoly situation' or what is meant by 'attributable to a monopoly situation', and other matters. It is not appropriate to deal with those in detail now, but it is a most unsatisfactory position where the Monopolies Commission has said things which meant that if it had stuck to the letter of the Act, it would not have been permitted to proceed. The judges' reaction to judicial review in relation to the Monopolies Commission is essentially non-interventionist. As a result, sloppy and unfair procedures, and some astonishing conclusions, can go forward insulated from any judicial challenge.

So we have a void in terms of reviewing the Commission's reports. These are not matters which are susceptible to Parliamentary review or to judicial review. That is a very unhappy and unfortunate position.

As the Chairman also said, the procedure is inquisitorial. But of course the Director General has started the action. More often than not, the whole inquiry has got off the ground because of a series of complaints from people who have brought the situation to the attention of the Director General to do something about it. He then determines that the inquiry should get underway. So in that sense it has been adversarial.

It has always been a source of some amazement to me that the Director General has no real rôle in the inquiry other than to determine that it should be referred. I am not aware of the Director General ever having given evidence – I may be wrong and I hope to be corrected.The Director General has started the show on the road, his team have done their investigation and determined there was something wrong, but other than at the level of an informal get-together between staff, and perhaps an introductory briefing for panel members, there is no continuing rôle for the Director General in the inquiry proceedings. I think that is wrong. He has the insight as to why it should have been investigated, why there was a *prima facie* case, if you like. He ought to have a rôle, an important one, in putting forward and justifying the reference. In other words, there is a strong adversarial element in these inquisitorial proceedings which ought to be recognised and not just waved away. There would not be any compromise to integrity or independence in the inquiry. The Director General would be an important witness.

The MMC's Inquiries – Too Much Confidentiality?

The inquiries themselves are, I think properly, conducted in private. These are not open sessions. But there is, I think, an over-emphasis upon confidentiality. By this I mean that a company under investigation will not see the evidence submitted by other people which may be damning it for its practices and their consequences. It is true that an important function of the Commission is to attempt to articulate those complaints and to put them back to the individuals, sometimes in the course of the oral hearings. But the oral hearings are relatively short in the context of an investigation. A major company under investigation with great commercial issues at stake may get, perhaps, two days in the course of what can be a 12- or 13-month reference. Now, that is not a long time to go over the material and put forward an argument to the Commissioners. And it is not always the case (I make no criticism because I understand the pressures) that all five Commissioners will be there. It is really not good enough to reply 'the Commissioners read the transcript'. Anybody who has read a transcript will know how difficult it is to understand what is going on in a hearing, and generally speaking, how incredibly boring and demanding it can be.

There is a case, it seems to me, while preserving privacy and certainly commercial confidentiality, that the submissions, which are overwhelmingly in writing to the Commission, should be made available to those whose commercial interests are at stake. There is nothing particularly controversial or radical about this; anybody with any experience of the EC Commission will know that if you make a complaint, either a formal complaint or a complaint for interim measures, it is absolutely essential that the contents of that complaint, in fact usually the document itself, will go to the party complained of. If there are secret business matters, they will be cut out. But, for the rest, the substance of the complaint and the evidence on which it is based will be made known to the parties involved. That seems to work perfectly well.

Call for Full-Time Commissioners

Turning now to the Commissioners. It is very difficult in the main not to have great admiration for the Commissioners. They are part-time and lay, and certainly in comparison with sister institutions, such as the EC Commission, the US Federal Trade Commission or the Department of Justice, Australia, New Zealand, the German Cartel Authority, which of course has jurisdiction over monopolies (as opposed to the German Monopolies Commission which has no jurisdiction over anything), they are (and I do not mean this in a pejorative sense) amateurs. In England that is a compliment. They, of course, draw from their own experience and they would not be there unless they had that experience, and that is important. But when all is said and done, these are major issues of immense importance to the companies concerned. If, as in the other jurisdictions I have mentioned, greater commitment both in time and professional background is deemed to be necessary, maybe we have overdone the lay element. I do not say the lay element is not important and that I would wish to do away with it, but this perhaps dovetails with the earlier idea of more full-time individuals who have perhaps special knowledge of competition.

In Germany, of course, it is very much an official and legal approach. I am not particularly suggesting that officials and lawyers should crowd the MMC, but I think there is scope. I think we may have overdone the 1940s vision of well-informed, high-minded individuals who know the public interest when they see it. I put it no higher than that.

There is also a pronounced shortage of entrepreneurs in all quangos. This is understandable. All quangos (I use the word non-pejoratively) have difficulty in getting self-employed people, active professionals, or people running their own business, as opposed to people in large organisations and public enterprises. But it is precisely the person with

17

that sort of background – the person starting a business who has been excluded and abused – who is liable to have rubbed up against monopolies.

An interesting development has been the recruitment of individuals from companies who have themselves been through a Monopolies Commission inquiry. These are people who by definition know all about an inquiry because they have been through it, and all about what monopolists can do. Otherwise they would not have been investigated. This is interesting and welcome.

How to Define the 'Public Interest'?

Lastly, I turn to the formulation of the public interest itself. It derives from post-war ambiguity about competition. We all know the exchange when Harold Wilson (then President of the Board of Trade) was asked in the House of Commons what the public interest was. He replied, without blinking, that he would know when he saw it. Now, there is an element of truth in that. Section 84 of the Fair Trading Act lists every conceivable ingredient of the public interest and could hardly ever be described as restrictive. The very breadth of the formula has the effect that it actually becomes very difficult to exclude evidence, particularly at the outset of an inquiry, because everything is potentially relevant under the tests. And nobody can say with any conviction that something is irrelevant. And this, I think, is one ingredient in the extreme zest for information that all parties to an inquiry experience.

The main feature which draws a line between the British approach to the abuse of dominant position and that of nearly every other jurisdiction is the complete absence of any compensatory remedy. The only form of remedy is prospective; that is to say, the Secretary of State may make an order or extract undertakings. In that process there is, again, a peculiarity because by that time the ball has passed typically to the Department of Trade and Industry or the Office of Fair Trading. Increasingly, the DTI is taking an important rôle in negotiating at least the first stages of an undertaking and then passing the ball to the Office of Fair Trading.

There is, therefore, a third stage in the whole inquiry – Director General's reference, the inquiry itself and then a further period with the officials at the DTI. This is a further opportunity for extensive lobbying, as all of us who have seen it first-hand know, and where politicians can become involved. The peculiarity of which I spoke is that the MMC – which has of course heard all the evidence, read it all, assimilated it and published extracts from it in its report – is not consulted, I am told, by the DTI as to the form of the undertakings or order or remedy that should finally be adopted. Those who have heard the evidence are not consulted, but the

Director General of Fair Trading, who has not heard the evidence, is consulted.

Judicial Review of MMC Reports

My last point is the complete lack of any judicial supervision. There have been many attempts to review MMC reports and MMC practices. As any member of the MMC will tell you, all of them have been unsuccessful. The score is at least 12-nil. It is now, I think, clear that the judges do not really want to know and that Mr Odgers and his colleagues would have to do something extremely out of character to elicit the interest of Her Majesty's judges.

As a result, an important element of quality control is missing. I have noticed over the last few years how very much the quality of EC Commission decisions and processes have improved. I attribute that directly, without any doubt whatsoever, to the rôle played by the Court of First Instance in the European Communities which, instead of just ticking decisions, as the old Court of Justice tended to do, is now going through the evidence, line by line, analysis by analysis, retaining its own experts and essentially second guessing the Commission's decision *if there are grounds to do so*. That has made a profound impact upon the quality of the decision-making of the Commission. In other words, judicial review is perhaps also an important element of quality control.

After these key factors, I want to end on a low note, on the EC Commission and the EC law itself. As you all know, Articles 85 and 86 are directly effective. If somebody comes into an adviser and says, 'I've got a problem, we're faced with a Monopoly Commission inquiry', several emotions go through an adviser's mind, but blind fear of the consequences is not one of them. That is no reflection on the Monopolies Commission. If somebody came in and said, 'the EC Commission is investigating', then there *is* a problem. It is much more serious. One factor is the prospect of a 10 per cent of turnover fine. The increased willingness of the Commission to levy very large fines indeed is a major problem for many companies. Allied to that, increasingly, there is the prospect of securing damages in a national court, with the encouragement of the Commission, to abate, or prevent, certain abuses of dominant position.

I see actions for injunctions in the English High Court as very much the way of the future, compared with lengthy investigations, or action under Article 86, even with all the reluctance judges have. Such action is increasingly being seen. In 1994, in my own experience, a letter before action was written on 29 April, we were in Court in mid-July having had extensive affidavit evidence exchanged in the interim period, and a six-day hearing. I am pleased to say the plaintiff got the remedy he wanted – an injunction. The alternatives which were canvassed at the beginning of that action were either to press for a Monopolies Commission reference, or to lodge a complaint with the Director General of Fair Trading, or a complaint, even, to Brussels. All those were rejected in favour of a High Court action.

For all its faults and for all the reluctance of the judges, this is an important development and one which I think will continue, because it guarantees a remedy in a reasonably clear time-frame. It remedies a major weakness in our legislative structure, namely, the refusal to grasp that if certain practices can be identified in advance, they can be proscribed. If, with all the evidential burden discharged, they are shown to exist then they should give rise to an action for damages and for injunction.

2

WATER: THE PERIODIC
REVIEW PROCESS

Ian Byatt
Ofwat

I PROPOSE TO EXAMINE THE PROCESSES of economic regulation in the water industry, particularly the process developed for the recent Periodic Review.

The Importance of Good Process

By process, I mean the *arrangements* for setting prices, the *consultation* on issues and explanation of decisions, the *involvement* of relevant parties, and *decision-taking* by the regulator. A process may be good or bad. Clausewitz defined war as 'the continuation of politics with the admixture of other means'. I think that the 'admixture of other means' should be kept to a minimum.

Orderly processes, where those concerned know what is to be settled, how it is to be settled and where surprises are avoided, obviate unnecessary conflict and unproductive argument. Recognition of good process and understanding of a situation usually provide an adequate framework for productive behaviour.

Utility regulators receive little guidance from the Act or from the Licence. Their governing Act tells them to 'act in the manner they consider best calculated ...'. A Licence is often explicit on what regulators should do in certain circumstances, for example, their governing in water, adjusting price limits when construction prices diverge from what was expected. It sometimes gives guidance of the kind of calculations to be carried out. Rarely is anything said about the *process* to be followed.

Criteria for Good Processes

I have sought to establish processes which are:

- Transparent: those involved should understand the issues, possess relevant information and be consulted.

- Fair: those involved should know how things are being decided and have a chance to present their arguments.

- Defensible: the basis and context of key decisions should be set out. Those involved should know why things have been decided and thus how they are likely to be decided in the future.

Transparent Process

In the case of water, those involved fall into the three main groups – the customers who pay the bills, those who want to see improvements in the water environment, and the companies who must deliver the goods. Each group is composed of sub-groups with different interests. For example, low- and high-income customers may have different views about improving (and paying for) higher quality and more expensive services. There are also regional disparities.

There is little scope for market processes to reflect individual preferences. Statements of preference – for example, for higher standards or lower bills – are helpful only if subject to budget constraints; in other words, if they are not influenced by the hope that a free lunch is round the corner.

Real information, properly communicated, is a scarce commodity in contrast to half-truths, sensational stories and downright misrepresentation. Knowledge, presentation and understanding all fall short of what we would like. Resources – particularly the time those listening can spare – are limited.

Targeting is needed. It is necessary to use the media, while recognising that it has agendas of its own. The hostility of those who cannot believe that anything good can come out of what they regard as an imperfect situation has to be faced.

Paying for Water

We at Ofwat have used different approaches in different areas. In our consultation on *Paying for Water* (1990) we adopted an ambitious strategy, attempting to reach a wide audience. The key points were in the main paper; there were annexes for experts. A leaflet was produced for wide circulation and a video was made. Public meetings were arranged to discuss the options. The Office of Population Censuses & Surveys (OPCS) carried out an opinion survey. Water companies agreed to put leaflets in their bills with a questionnaire for return to Ofwat.

On the basis of the response to this consultation, *Paying for Water: The*

Way Ahead (1991) was published, setting out my conclusions. This has been the basis of Ofwat policy since then. But it remains necessary to remind people regularly of these conclusions.

Cost of Capital and Assessing Capital Value

The consultation on the *Cost of Capital* (1991) was directed to a more specialist audience. It was linked with consultation on the base to which the cost of capital should be applied – *Assessing Capital Values at the Periodic Review* (1992). Both these papers had an impact in the City and led to a number of substantial responses, providing a framework for subsequent discussions with the City – discussions which continued right up to the receipt of Strategic Business Plans (SBPs) last Easter.

We also consulted on *Paying for Growth* (1993). In the case of regulated industries where customers pay according to use, companies can finance the cost of the additional output from higher sales. In the case of customers taking an unmeasured supply, the cost of additional supplies can be financed only from higher prices.

Cost of Quality

Consultation on quality was very extensive. It involved two major papers in successive years – *The Cost of Quality* (1992) and *Paying for Quality* (1993).

The *Cost of Quality* paper drew people's attention to the possible impact on bills of the drive towards higher quality on the basis of two scenarios. *Paying for Quality* took the process further on the basis of costings by water companies – costings which had been validated by the independent Reporters appointed under the Licence and exposed to the Department of the Environment (DoE), the Drinking Water Inspectorate (DWI) and the National Rivers Authority (NRA). We put effort into drawing these matters to the attention of a wide audience. (We even appeared on page 7 of the *Daily Sport.*)

The *Paying for Quality* consultation was not simply a matter of raising issues. The published document was an open letter to the Secretaries of State for the Environment and for Wales, urging them to recognise the impact quality obligations could have on customers' bills and, indeed, to moderate that impact by considering deferral of some of the deadlines of the EC Urban Waste Water Treatment Directive (UWWTD).

This was a major step in the Periodic Review. The response from the Secretaries of State provided clear guidance on the legally enforceable quality obligations to be allowed for in price limits. It also led to substantial reductions in costs and bills compared with what otherwise could have happened. This arose mainly as a result of decisions about how policies, such as the EC UWWTD, were to be implemented.

Market Plans and Discretionary Levels of Service

Ofwat also stimulated consultation on the provision of discretionary services, going beyond legally enforceable obligations. Companies were encouraged to produce Market Plans in the Spring and early Summer of 1993, which would set out options for their customers, and to buttress this with market research. The plans provided the vehicle for consulting customers generally – as opposed to representative bodies. Market research can secure views from a cross-section of customers and not just from the vociferous. This work indicated customers' priorities among the different services provided by water companies.

We have also sought to attract wider interest through press notices, summaries and leaflets. There are 30 Information Notes explaining the regulatory arrangements. There is a series of background leaflets. (One I am particularly proud of tells people how much it costs to use water for activities such as bathing and using the lavatory.)

Fair Process

I have sought, to the extent possible, to set out in advance the criteria which would be used in regulatory decisions. Before exercising powers on first-time rural sewerage, I published an Information Note setting out the approach I would take. When, in the Competition and Service (Utilities) Act 1992, Parliament said that water companies should trade with their group companies at arm's length, I issued a consultation paper on how transfer pricing issues would be approached.

It is not always possible fully to set out criteria and methods of administration at an early stage of a policy. Perceptions may change – quite rightly – as issues become clearer, or new issues arise. If so, guidance notes need to be revised.

Indicating criteria and the process for considering issues and making decisions is part of natural justice. It also helps people to decide what cases they might bring to the regulator – and what they might try to settle in other ways. Out-of-court settlements can involve less resources. The clearer the expectations both parties have of the results of going to the regulator, the more likely it is that a satisfactory agreement can be made by the parties themselves.

For the Periodic Review, we put considerable effort into establishing processes with the quality regulators and with the Government, as well as with the companies. I will take these in turn.

Approach to Periodic Review

Having issued various consultation papers (Green Papers), we pulled all our thoughts together in a White Paper, *Setting Price Limits for Water and Sewerage Services; the framework and approach to the Periodic Review* (1993), published well in advance of the main quantitative work involved in setting K factors. I thought the companies, the customers and other interested parties (such as the City) should know how the job would be done.

On the day when price limits were determined and announced I published a 58-page document, *Future charges for water and sewerage services; the outcome of the Periodic Review*. This explained the reasons behind the decisions and linked the quantitative results of the Review with the qualitative approach set out the previous November. (On that day, Eamonn Butler from the Adam Smith Institute, commenting on the determinations, said that 'you need the regulator to give reasons for these things'. What, I wonder, was he trying to tell us?)

Quality Regulators and Government

When the original K factors were set in 1989, there was much talk of imposition of further quality and environmental standards, and of 'cost pass through' into prices. This did not take long to become a reality. In 1990 the then Minister, Chris Patten, had imposed new obligations by accelerating the Bathing Waters programme and by some anticipation of the new EC UWWTD. I warned that this would involve a substantial increase in bills, especially in the South West, where the company already had high K factors and high bills. In due course the Patten initiative led to an increase of South West's factor from 6·5 to 11·5.

This intensified my desire to strengthen the regulatory mechanisms. During 1992, the arguments for adequate costing, and full consideration of costs, before decisions were made, began to prevail. Ofwat's paper, *The Cost of Quality*, took the issue on to the national stage.

Tripartite and Quadripartite Machinery

Following this, Quadripartite (that is, DoE, NRA, Ofwat and the companies) activity developed under the aegis of the DoE. This machinery proved very effective during 1993 and 1994. The DoE set out its approach as the standard-setter in *Water Charges: the Quality Framework*. This contained clear guidance to the Director on the quality obligations which he should take into account when setting price limits. The quality regulators and the companies developed guidelines, where standards were related to detailed implementation. These guidelines were then costed. Initially they were used for setting out options – as in *Paying for Quality*. After the publication of *Water Charges: the Quality Framework*, the guidelines were developed to implement the agreed quality framework, so that they could be used in the Strategic Business Plans which the companies were to submit in March 1994.

This Quadripartite machinery, under the excellent chairmanship of Neil Summerton, provides an effective link between my task, as an independent regulator, to ensure that the companies can finance legally enforceable quality obligations and the Secretaries of State's responsibility for setting quality and environmental standards. It links the formulation of policy for a sector of the economy to the implementation of that policy. It has enabled good and productive working relationships to be developed between Ofwat and the quality regulators, the NRA and the DWI.

This is the *institutional logic* behind the disaggregation of the RPI + K factor into RPI −X +Q, where Q is the cost of quality.

Relations with the Companies

I think it highly desirable to have a range of continuing contacts with the regulated companies, with varying degrees of formality. We have, therefore:

(i) set up working groups with the companies. There are three major groups on issues ranging from regulatory accounts to investment policy. Membership is by my invitation, but I am careful to choose those who can speak to important interests of the companies;

(ii) arranged annual meetings with each company, where I meet the Managing Director and discuss regulatory strategy. In addition, there is a good deal of contact on day-to-day matters between company staff and Ofwat officials;

(iii) arranged seminars and workshops with representatives of all the companies to discuss regulatory developments and the contents of Ofwat consultation papers;

(iv) written regularly to companies setting out the processes we propose to follow. These letters to Managing Directors are also publicly available. For example, I wrote in March 1992 (MD 72) setting out Ofwat's analytic approach to the Periodic Review and in September 1993 (MD 96) setting out the process I intended to follow;

(v) suggested individual meetings in January and February 1994, to ensure that regulator and company understood each other's positions and to facilitate the work of submitting and assessing the companies' Strategic Business Plans.

Submission of Strategic Business Plans (SBP), Draft Determinations and Due Process Meetings

The Periodic Review process was carefully planned and set out in advance. The information required by the Director under the Licence took the form of a SBP (which Richard Briant, in the manner of Gibbon, said was neither strategic nor about business, nor a plan, but a bid for resources). This set out what obligations the companies must meet, the service they proposed to provide for their customers and the price limits they considered necessary to finance the proper carrying out of these functions.

We also set out the stages of the determination: the issue of a draft determination, the timetable for sending in written representations, the due process meeting for the Director to listen to representations and to understand key points, and the arrangements for announcing the final determinations and informing the companies. (*Inter alia*, I stressed that K setting was *not* a process of negotiation.)

There were issues involving the handling of sensitive information, where we were in close touch with the Stock Exchange. I think some aspects of confidentiality need careful exploration before the next Review.

Relations with Customers

I think it is also highly desirable to have a range of continuing contacts with consumer bodies.

My most significant contacts on the customer side are with the Customer Service Committees (CSCs) and particularly with their Chairmen. As an integral part of Ofwat, Chairmen have access to the resources of the Office. They speak from a position of knowledge.

● I established a Chairmen's Group in 1990 which met about six times a year. Discussions in this group have ranged widely across the work of the Office, covering regulatory matters concerning both the DG's statutory duties and customer matters and concerning the statutory duties of the CSCs.

- In 1993, the Chairmen's Group evolved into the Ofwat National Customer Council (ONCC). This is chaired by Jim Gardner, one of the Chairmen. ONCC is rapidly developing a rôle of its own.

- I involved the Chairmen closely in the price setting process last Summer. They had access to the SBPs of the companies allocated to their CSCs. They saw the confidential reports I sent to the companies with their draft determinations. They saw their companies' representations and attended the meetings with their companies. Before making my final decisions, I had informed advice from each of the CSC Chairmen. This was a major regulatory innovation.

- I also maintain contact with other consumer bodies. I regularly speak to Judith Wilcox, Chairman of the National Consumer Council. Ofwat attends meetings of the Public Utilities Access Forum, which represents the interests of customers disadvantaged by low income or poor health. We are in touch with the National Association of Citizens Advice Bureaux and the Consumers' Association.

Many MPs are interested in the regulation of the water companies and I have tried always to be accessible to them. I have appeared once, in five years, before the Commons Select Committee on the Environment and once gave evidence to a Select Committee of the Lords. The relationship is a developing one. There are some constitutional issues involved, which are for Parliament and Government rather than the regulator to advance.

Explanation of Decisions

I vigorously contest the canard, which regularly waddles out, that regulators do not give reasons. I doubt if it was ever true; it is certainly not true as far as the economic regulation of the water companies is concerned.

Explanation must take place in several layers. At one level the arguments need to be set out rigorously and with sufficient detail to make the position clear. In the case of my most important set of decisions, this was done in two publications – *Setting Price Limits for Water and Sewerage Services: the Framework and Approach to the Periodic Review* (November 1993), and *Future Charges for Water and Sewerage Services; the outcome of the Periodic Review* (July 1994). The methods and the answers will, of course, be further tested when the MMC comes to set price limits for South West Water and Portsmouth Water.

Only a small proportion of those concerned read these publications. So, on the day of the announcement, we paid much attention to presentation through the media. I was glad to be able to tell the *Today* audience about the new price limits at the same time as they were shown on the Stock Exchange screens. We issued a leaflet for the general public.

We arranged presentations for the Press and for the City analysts, where I set out, in a 10-minute presentation, the key elements in the announcement and answered questions for the next hour. I was available to (and was used by) TV and radio programmes during the day. Our media day ran almost continuously from 7.30 a.m. to 11.30 p.m. In the regions, the CSC Chairmen took the burden of explaining my decisions. The Chairmen had also published their views.

An acid test of explanations is whether anyone listens. I felt that, in the media coverage of the new price limits, there was some understanding of what Ofwat had done and what its rôle and powers were. To be criticised for not having done what we had no powers to do can be galling, but it does provide an opportunity to set out the rôle of the regulator – which is, ultimately, a matter for Parliament.

Conclusions

Regulation of privatised utilities has developed its own debate. But although there is much discussion of regulation, there is less understanding of the rôle of regulators, of their powers and how their work relates to other national objectives. Despite the interest in them as individuals, there is little objective discussion of the processes they have developed to carry out the duties imposed on them.

The debate would be richer if more objective research were available to provide a better basis for appraisal. I hope that research workers in universities and research institutes will rise to the challenge. In this talk I have tried to set out some facts.

Arrangements for ordering the collective life of human beings are inevitably complex. The aggressive tendencies of the human animal have to be channelled and, sometimes, curbed. In economic life this usually comes down to some balance of incentives, competition and regulation. It is rarely possible to specify the correct balance in the abstract. We learn to get these things right as much through experience as through ratiocination.

I will leave the last word with Lemuel Gulliver who wrote:

'.... Providence never intended to make the management of public affairs a mystery to be comprehended only by a few persons of sublime genius, of which there seldom are three born in an age; but they suppose truth, justice, temperance and the like, to be in every man's power; the practice of which virtues assisted by experience and a good intention, would qualify every man for the service of his country, except where a course of study is required.'[1]

CROWN COPYRIGHT RESERVED

1 Jonathan Swift, *Gulliver's Travels*, Part I: *A Voyage to Lilliput* (1726), quoted from the Penguin English Library Edition, 1967, reprinted in Penguin Classics, 1985, pp. 95-96.

DISCUSSANT'S COMMENTS

Dr Dieter Helm
Fellow of New College, Oxford

I WILL KEEP my replies brief, will try to measure up to the Chairman's introductory remarks by introducing controversy, and will try to cover some of the points raised in Ian Byatt's presentation, though I did not have the opportunity of reading it in advance. He did say, by the way, that it would not make much difference, and I suppose that is an example of where regulation is self-fulfilling.

British Regulation: Three Negatives

Let me start with general remarks and then go on to some points of detail. The British system of regulation, of which water regulation is an important part, was designed with three negative points in mind: explicitly to reject rate of return regulation, US style; to reject government control of utilities; and to reject for most of the utilities at least the assumption of monopoly. Thus price caps, independent regulators with discretion, and the promotion of competition were born.

In due course I suspect we will hear more about the promotion of competition in water, but it is with the first two that we are primarily concerned. The core question that we can now begin to address is how has the discretion at the heart of independent regulation been exercised in the two great major reviews, in electricity and water – the latter my concern in this commentary. We need to address that in terms of the process with which Ian has dealt in some considerable detail, and in terms of the outcome. A process at the end of the day should be fair, transparent, and defensible, but what really matters is whether this sort of utility regulation is producing results which are consistent with efficient utilities and a balance which delivers the benefits fairly between consumers and shareholders.

The Process

Let me begin with process, because that was at the heart of Ian's presentation, and understandably so given the cases which are now pending before the Monopolies and Mergers Commission.

We now have a chance to reflect on how different regulators have used their discretion, in particular on the regulatory styles which now emerge. Contrast, if you will, the conduct of Ian Byatt in the Water Periodic Review with the conduct of Stephen Littlechild in the Electricity Review. They are fundamentally different. Ian Byatt has described a process which is about as open and transparent as one could possibly get within the British regulatory system without being wide open to judicial review at each and every stage. It is very hard to find fault with the careful setting out of, first, cost of capital discussion papers, then asset valuation discussion papers, the discussion of the cost of quality and, of course, the two papers at the end on setting the price limits and the outcome – the decision. That has been a very logical, very clear and thoroughly laudable process, which it is very hard to criticise.

Contrast that with electricity. Have we had discussion papers on the cost of capital, on asset valuation? Have we had clear discussions as to why the Capex level is going to be so high for the regional electricity companies for the next five years? Have we had the detailed set of reasons for the decisions given? Not a bit of it! On the contrary, it is very hard to work out how the asset value was set for the regional electricity companies; how it was set for the Scottish companies; how those two relate together and how they relate to the British Gas MMC case.

And that has been a matter of choice. Nobody forced Ian Byatt to produce those discussion papers. They are not required in the legislation or the licences. He chose that path and Stephen Littlechild chose a different one. Subsequent regulators can choose their own path to follow in future decisions. And the difference in the detail is fantastic too. Contrast the strategic business plans, the scrutiny of the Capex programmes, the comparative efficiency exercises that Ofwat have conducted with those of Offer and you will find a marked gulf. Again, that was a matter of choice.

So, in terms of process, it is hard to think of a more detailed process, or a more open process, or a more transparent one than we have had in the water case. And I think that in exercising that discretion a considerable amount of praise is due to the Director General in the case of water.

Outcome

But we also have to turn to the outcome of the process and, to be fair to Offer, to a rather different view on what periodic review is about. The thousands of pages that we had on the strategic business plans, compared to the few pages we had from Offer, reflect a different view of what a regulator is doing. In neither case do the outcomes appear immediately (though it is still very early to tell) to have struck an enduring balance between the shareholders and the customers.

Early indications of abnormal returns not only to the Regional Electricity Companies (RECs) in particular, but also the water companies, indicate that the balance, if anything, has gone the shareholders' way. Add to that the City comment about dividend growth and about future performance, summarised (I think rather unfairly) in one publication which had the headline 'Utilities 2 Regulators 0', and it all suggests that the balance has not come out perfectly.

What do we conclude from that? It is very hard to think that more effort could have gone into it, or more detail. I do not think that another thousand pages of strategic business plans would have got us closer to the right result. It seems to me inevitable in this system that the results will be wrong if less detail is engaged in, the result may be worse, and perhaps shown in the difference between the REC's share price and the water companies' gains, though it is very early days.

That raises the question as to whether there should be an error-correction mechanism. Basically we are told in water and electricity: 'Well, I may have got it right or I may have got it wrong, but we'll talk about that in the year 2000', or perhaps even in the year 2005 in the case of water. (I do not believe that is an enduring possibility in the RECs' case. There I believe intervention will follow.)

But, in trying to preserve the characteristic of the price cap, which is essentially different from rate of return regulation only in so far as it introduces a lag, we have to accept that if you get the result wrong, then the prices will be out of equilibrium for a long time. The onus on those people who fix the prices and leave them alone must be that they must feel they can get it roughly right.

We have, of course, the cost pass-through interim determination mechanism, but that is very narrow. We do not have a mechanism for dealing with a misjudgement about the rates of return, resulting in abnormal returns to the utilities. Ian Byatt has made the point in his discussion papers very clearly, that he does not seek to intervene. He seeks to leave this cap alone, to let the efficiency incentives work out.

Credibility of Price Caps

Two questions about that arise. In rate of return regulation we have the same variables – Opex, Capex, asset value and rate of return – as in the periodic review. But for the price cap incentives to work, we have to ask whether it is actually credible. Do investors and companies believe that these price caps will be left alone until the year 2000 before intervention?

And, as I have pointed out elsewhere, the evidence about the likelihood of that being credible, from the first five years of electricity privatisation, is very different from the evidence of the first five years of water. In electricity there was enormous pressure to intervene. Stephen Littlechild stuck rigorously to the principle of non-intervention on the argument it would be put right at the periodic review. (As an aside, it has not been.)

In water, the formula has been repeatedly affected by interventions from the regulator under pressure from political parties, from customers, broadly politicians from a large number of groups who have demanded intervention. We have had voluntary price cuts, price cuts under the threat of interim determinations, and changes to the Capex. That may or may not be desirable. My point is simply that if you have a history of intervening, it is not very credible in the next period to say you are not going to do so, particulary if the result turns out not to be spot on.

There is a particular reason why intervention seems to me to be likely, namely, that we still have no really solid basis for agreeing the criteria for establishing what Capex ought to be. John Kay referred to this, linking it back to procedures the Treasury used previously. To the extent that question is not answered, it is going to be revisited, giving quite a lot of scope for disturbance, separate from the scope for disturbance that comes from the abnormal returns.

The Public Interest

The second question is whether it is in the public interest to leave the formula alone until the year 2000 or 2005. The standard reply is 'yes', because that is the only thing that gives us the efficiency incentives. And I think there are two replies to that: one a point of principle and one pragmatic.

In competitive markets, firms do not have prices fixed for five years and left alone; they are subject to price shocks. Nothing in competitive markets protects firms from these for periods of time. There is no argument that firms like ICI should be immune from the shocks because otherwise they would give up trying to be efficient. ICI would not bleat that it cut down its efficiency incentive drives because the recession hit it and cut prices in final markets.

Also, as I have argued, the prices will not be left alone anyway. Does one have a mechanism within the framework of our regulatory system which allows errors to be corrected, or does one wait for the politicians to pull it all down? The political reaction may be to throw out the whole régime, or appoint a regulator who is more like-minded, or to impose windfall taxes.

The Conservatives have given the Labour Party the degree of discretion for intervention in the utilities that they gave the Labour Party through the 1972 Industry Act to intervene in industry more generally between 1974 and 1979. If one went through the thought experiment of choosing a regulator for electricity from the ranks of the Labour Party who has experience in the electricity sector, say an ex-Secretary of State like Tony Benn, and one asked what he could do with those powers, the answer would be a great deal.

I suspect the politicians will make speeches about changing the regulatory régime, windfall taxes and intervention. In the meantime, the Regulator will try as hard as he can to keep the companies on the straight and narrow, and see how the excess dividends can be spent, in ways which keep the overall return down. There will be arm twisting and intervention between periodic reviews. The price cap may stay intact, but the reality below the formula will be changed and will affect incentives for efficiency.

Conclusions

My first conclusion is that one needs to think about how well it meets the overall objectives of the regulatory system. Has it really escaped the characteristics of US regulation it was designed to avoid?

But the big test is the one Christopher Foster has raised – is it open to regulatory capture? Capture is usually described as a process by which regulators end up acting in the interest of regulatees. If the perception is that shareholders do well under such systems, that regulators act in the interest of shareholders, in the water, but particularly in the electricity case, it is very hard to see how shareholders could have been left with higher rates of return. There is no evidence that this system is less captured in shareholder interest than the US system. But we should not throw the system out, we should reform it, and build on what we have. I have suggested some kind of error-correction mechanism, which does not throw out all the efficiency incentives, but rather enables the system to correct obvious mistakes when they become manifest.

At the end of the day, the main conclusion is that in the British system what regulation you get depends on who is doing it. Under the Byatt régime, we have had a very open and procedurally correct process: the best that any of the utility regulators has achieved. It is very hard to think how one could do better. Nevertheless, the outcome has not necessarily been one which leaves the system sustainable. If we do not reform it, the politicians are waiting in 1997 to think of more draconian solutions. It has not, as yet, become acceptable either politically or to customers.

35

INTERCONNECT:
HOW REGULARORY OBJECTIVES
SHOULD BE MET

Alan Bell

Oftel

Introduction

I WANT TO OUTLINE WHAT OFTEL IS DOING in the context of interconnection policy, to provide some background to this work, to explore issues of appropriate interconnection charges, and then to discuss some of OFTEL's key objectives in this area.

This is an appropriate time to talk about interconnection in the UK telecommunications sector. OFTEL is about to publish a consultative paper[1] dealing with a number of issues all related in one way or another to interconnection. I focus here on some of the tricky underlying issues related to economic aspects of interconnection and to link these in a general way to OFTEL's objectives. I do not propose to come to any firm conclusions but rather expose some of the underlying thinking.

You will, of course, be aware that interconnection has been the major regulatory issue for OFTEL over the last two years. There is no question that it will continue to be so over the next year or two. In addition, full liberalisation of network services is scheduled for 1998 and the Commission in Brussels is doing a good deal to ensure that there is an appropriate interconnection régime in place. It is also preparing a document on infrastructure competition. We find ourselves, therefore, working in harmony in Europe.

Background

Before moving into some of the more detailed and complex issues on interconnection, perhaps I can begin with a brief account of the position that has been reached on competition, which is what interconnection in

---

[1] *Editor's Note:* published as *A Framework for Effective Competition*, Oftel, December 1994.

telecoms is really all about. To put the interconnection issue into perspective, I need to go back to the Duopoly Review of 1990-91. You will recall that its aim was to explore whether or not to continue the policy of licensing only two public telephone operators - BT and Mercury - in the UK.

The essential conclusions of the review about structural regulation were:

- to end the Duopoly policy and to encourage entry into all domestic markets through easy availability of licences (which are, of course, the responsibility of the DTI); and

- the maintenance of a kind of asymmetric regulatory régime, designed to limit BT's freedom to move, on the basis of its main licence, into new technologies and service offerings, for example, entertainment and wireless services, whilst at the same time allowing new entrants to provide such services. (BT is, however, entitled to compete for licences to deliver entertainment services on the same basis as other companies.)

The Duopoly Review therefore created a liberalised environment designed to encourage entry into the market, though less so on international services, which are something of a separate issue. You will gather from this, therefore, that the essential basis of the Duopoly Review was the expectation that competitive entry would be based on a variety of technologies including cable and wireless, the economics of which are different from those of a traditional wireline telecoms operator. These technologies would give new entrants a competitive advantage over incumbents in certain contexts.

As a result of the liberalisation policy, around 50 PTO licences have been issued. Another 40 applications are pending. These operators will be offering a wide range of services from niche value-added services to a full range of PTO services. I will make some reference to these other services later on. It is perhaps worth re-emphasising here that one of the key underlying aims of the Duopoly Review was to encourage network or infrastructure competition: it had less of an impact on competition from service providers, which was already liberalised. However, despite the advent of a régime with fairly free entry, the fact remains that BT continues to be in an extremely powerful position in the provision of UK telecoms services, having as many as 25 million UK customers on its network. It is estimated, for example, that around 97 per cent of all calls made in the United Kingdom touch BT's network at some point. It follows from this, therefore, that interconnection with BT by other operators is absolutely critical if competition is to develop in the UK.

Present Activities

Under the current interconnection régime, the situation is broadly that an operator can either make a private commercial deal with BT or, if it fails to do so, then one or both parties apply to OFTEL for a determination. This requirement is necessary to achieve the 'any to any' principle - a subscriber on one network should have access to subscribers on all other networks. In making such a determination OFTEL is constrained in what it can do by the provisions laid down in BT's licence. These provisions prescribe that the price of interconnection which OFTEL determines should be based on BT's fully allocated costs.

At the end of the Duopoly Review, some amendments were made to the regulatory régime, in particular to the relevant parts of BT's licence, to allow for the impact of greater competition. These amendments were primarily designed to ensure that in a situation where BT's prices are out of line with its costs, due in part to regulatory action, inefficient entry would be discouraged. At the same time, however, it gave a certain amount of discretion to OFTEL to assist new entrants in a way designed to overcome their initial disadvantages. For those familiar with the UK telecoms scene, this relates to the advent of access deficit contributions (ADCs) and to the ability of the Director General to grant waivers for the payment of ADCs by new entrants up to prescribed market shares.

With a large number of new entrants seeking to offer a wide range of services, it has become increasingly obvious that a full review of the interconnection régime is required. The current arrangements leave a good deal of discretion to OFTEL to decide who should get such assistance, and over what period. This not only places OFTEL in an invidious position in choosing how to deploy such assistance but also creates a good deal of uncertainty amongst operators as to whether such assistance will be available and for how long. This is a major factor driving the current review of the interconnection régime.

OFTEL's approach to these issues has taken two directions. *First*, to announce and carry through a programme of accounting separation for BT. The form of accounting separation pursued splits BT's systems business into network, retail and access. Separate accounts for these activities will be produced in 1995. In addition, there will be far greater transparency than hitherto in BT's cost allocation procedures through the publication of BT's cost drivers and a series of standard charges determined by OFTEL for components of BT's network. Account is taken of whether the services offered by BT are monopoly or competitive with those available elsewhere, and what new monopoly services might be added to the list of standard charges. The programme also addresses a range of related issues such as access to numbering arrangements, standardisation of contracts, availability of number portability and equal access, standardisation of network interfaces and the provision of market information. In addition, arrangements will be put in place to ensure no undue discrimination takes place between BT's treatment of its own business and its treatment of competitors.

The *second* element of the review will look at more fundamental, long-term questions concerning the basis on which interconnection charges should be set. It addresses issues of tariff rebalancing, universal service obligations, access deficit contributions and whether some form of interconnection arrangement based on capacity charging might be appropriate. These were the issues addressed in our December 1994 paper.[2]

A key part in the development of these new arrangements is being played by the operators, since an important mechanism is the holding of OFTEL/ industry and users' fora where all the various issues are discussed, thereby ensuring OFTEL initiatives are soundly based, appropriate and robust and, where possible, based on consensus.

It is primarily on the so-called longer term issues of interconnection charges that I want to focus in this paper. In doing so, I should point out that I am intending to describe a range of possible views and not those that OFTEL will adopt. Indeed, OFTEL will not reach any conclusions until the completion of the consultation period which the December paper inaugurated. An interconnection arrangement contains many elements, relating to the location of interconnection, technical standards, and so on. However, the least tractable has proved to be the setting of interconnection charges.

Setting Interconnection Charges

The setting of interconnection charges is clearly a multi-dimensional issue but assessment can be made more manageable by establishing at the outset some objectives that any form of interconnection charging régime might be expected to meet, although their relative importance may vary over time and from place to place. These objectives might be as follows:

● *The attainment of appropriate levels of prices, production and consumption of telecommunication services, or allocative efficiency.*

Interconnection charges are clearly an important element of cost in the provision of services and their level, like the price of any other

---

[2] *A Framework for Effective Competition*, OFTEL, December 1994.

input, is likely to influence service tariffs. They therefore have important resource implications.

- *The attainment of efficiency over time through technical innovation achieved through competitive pressures and incentives to operate efficiently, to invest appropriately and to innovate.*

The structure of the industry should ensure that customers benefit from proper levels of competition and choice in the provision of the final services and that operators enjoy the same benefits in the provision of interconnection. In particular, interconnection prices should be set at a level which avoids unnecessary duplication of networks but puts sufficient pressure on all operators to provide network services at minimum cost. Other things equal, if entrants have to pay high interconnection prices they will have to charge more for final services and will be encouraged to build their own networks to bypass the incumbent. Higher interconnection charges may even deter entrants from entering at all. Clearly, therefore, how interconnection charges are set is potentially an important instrument for structural regulation.

- *Allowing the incumbent to make a sufficient return to sustain the costs of social obligations.*

If an incumbent has to cross-subsidise particular services or particular customers because of regulatory requirements, it is inevitably vulnerable to cream-skimming entry. Although this may serve the goal of entry promotion in the short run, if left unchecked in the long term it could lead to problems in maintaining the incumbent's capacity to fund its social obligations.

These are, I think, the three conventional objectives of interconnection pricing. One of the key elements of interconnection policy is that the importance of the three objectives changes over time. During major changes in structure, the entry promotion objective may be important but when the industry settles to a more steady pattern, allocative efficiency may play a more important rôle.

Pricing for Efficiency

As far as the objective of allocative efficiency is concerned, the issue of how interconnection prices should be set has been widely discussed, although the problems of implementing particular solutions are still considerable.

From a first-best viewpoint, interconnection prices should ideally be set equal to marginal or incremental costs. As is well known, marginal cost pricing of inputs will encourage efficient pricing of final services. In addition, marginal cost pricing of all inputs will encourage sellers of final services to use them either singly or in an efficient combination.

However, the problem with this policy is that where there are economies of scale or scope, a uniform policy of marginal cost pricing will cause a network operator to incur losses on interconnection services it sells to others and those which it provides for itself. The general requirement that the incumbent must break even overall thus entails a departure from marginal cost pricing. What that departure might be depends to some extent on the degree of competition in final outputs between incumbent and competitor. It has been argued that, where the entrant is using its interconnection to the incumbent's network to provide a service which competes exactly with that of the incumbent, then the appropriate departure from marginal cost pricing for interconnection should be to set interconnection equal to the incumbent's final service price, less the incremental cost to the incumbent of providing the competitive input. The rationale for this rule is straightforward. With the price of final services set at the minimum practicable level (to cover total costs with no abnormal profit) it has been suggested that an entrant should only come into the market if its costs are less than the incremental costs of the incumbent's output which it replaces in the market. Because the rivals' outputs are one-to-one substitutes and there is no price competition, the only issue is cost minimisation. This is the so-called Efficient Component Pricing Rule (ECPR).

The ECPR, of course, makes no allowance for any inefficiency on the part of the incumbent. It is also a very harsh rule to apply in that new entrants have to beat the incremental costs of the incumbent. Accounting separation can, of course, help to explore the true costs of interconnection. It also needs to be recognised that using such an approach may lead to different operators having to pay different prices for interconnection, depending upon the market in which they operate and the opportunity cost they impose on the incumbent. Price discrimination of this kind makes it possible to recover common costs in a way which maintains competitive parity. It may, however, present unacceptable practical and presentational difficulties.

An alternative basis for setting interconnection charges is so-called Ramsey pricing. It was noted above that one of the aims of interconnection pricing is to promote efficiency in the prices and levels of consumption of final services. Efficient final services prices in a network industry like telecommunications, where there are economies of scale and scope, require mark-ups over marginal or incremental cost which are inversely proportionate to the price elasticity of demand of the service in question.[3] Thus overheads fall disproportionately on services demand for which is relatively insensitive to price. The efficient pattern of prices for final services should also be reflected in interconnection prices. This will mean in practice that interconnection prices are differentiated in accordance with the final service they help to provide. The more price-elastic demand for that final service is, the lower the interconnection price. It is clear that implementing such an arrangement requires knowledge of demand conditions and this could be complex and difficult to achieve.

I have mentioned static efficiency. However, it is clear that as far as the objective of dynamic efficiency is concerned (that is, the benefits from competition as a result of innovation, etc.), interconnection charges can play a major rôle in the promotion of entry. The argument here is that entry is socially desirable because it offers customers a choice and because it galvanises the incumbent to strive for greater efficiency; but it may be privately unprofitable without special intervention because of the barriers to entry created by economies of scale. Some lowering of interconnection charges for entrants may help to overcome this difficulty. Clearly, such a policy is only sustainable provided that the discounted benefits of more competition outweigh the immediate costs of subsidising operators to produce output which in the short term is more costly than that produced by the incumbent.

Social Obligations and Constraints on Retail Prices

It is well known that in setting its prices, BT is subject to a combination of regulatory constraints. In particular, it has a constraint on increases in its exchange line rental and a requirement for geographical averaging of prices. These constraints on retail prices may have the effect of making access unprofitable, although the enormous uncertainties in demand for telecoms services make it difficult to figure out how a profit-maximising operator would set prices. It seems likely that the averaging constraint has the effect of making certain classes of customers profitable and others unprofitable. Possibly unbalanced and certainly averaged tariffs open up the possibility of inefficient entry. How can this be addressed?

A number of mechanisms exist for sharing the costs of meeting the needs of unprofitable customers or services. Many of these mechanisms involve tampering with interconnection charges, the method being thought

---

3 More technically: the 'superelasticity' which incorporates cross-market effects.

desirable because it is easily understood and because it links another operator's contributions directly and automatically to its market share. When the costs of subsidising a particular service such as access are at issue, the access deficit can be regarded as a common cost or overhead for companies providing usage services. These common costs are then recovered in a way intended to avoid distortion in the industry structure. Similarly, when universal service obligations (USOs) at averaged tariffs impose burdens, the net costs of providing service to unprofitable customers can be shared amongst operators, possibly through the appropriate level of interconnection charges. OFTEL is aware of these problems and has recently commissioned some preliminary work on the costs of USOs. This work will feed in to the review process. A major consideration will be just how any USO costs might best be recovered. One approach could be to seek lowest bids from alternative operators including the incumbent.

A further issue of current interest is the use of so-called capacity charging arrangements for interconnection. This is a largely new concept for telecommunications, although there are precedents in electricity and gas. The principle underlying the concept is that, as the telecoms network is dimensioned to meet a level of expected capacity, charges for the use of the network should reflect calls on that capacity. Precisely what it might involve and the extent to which it are feasible are as yet not entirely clear. At one level it is simply about recovering capacity-related costs imposed on the network by an operator's use of capacity, whilst at another it is about operators jointly investing in capacity which they are then free to utilise. In some ways, capacity charging is about risk-sharing of network costs. Given the absence of precedent, OFTEL has commissioned a study designed to establish the feasibility of setting interconnection rates as the basis of some form of capacity charging, possibly in conjunction with other methods. It is the intention to share the findings with operators during the forthcoming consultation process.

Asset Values

Finally, I should like to touch on measurement issues, in particular whether interconnection charges should be forward-looking or based on historic cost. Most interconnection charging schemes start from incremental or direct costs. It is also part of their logic to measure such costs on a forward-looking as opposed to an historic cost accounts (HCA) basis. If interconnection charges are to provide the right signals to the incumbent and other operators, these should be set on a forward-looking basis using an efficient technology. This can be achieved either by the use of current cost accounts (CCA) in which assets are entered at their replacement value; or, alternatively, an approach based on engineering models might be appropriate, although there are grave practical difficulties here of estimating non-technology related costs. This suggests that the use of current cost accounts may represent a sensible compromise, combined with an efficiency test.

However, the issue of historic versus current cost accounts has very important implications for the retail price cap which is set on an historic cost basis. Any decisions to move towards current costs as the basis for setting interconnection charges would have to take account of the impact on the retail price cap. The possibility of OFTEL's regulating BT on a CCA basis was mooted at the time of the price control proposals in 1992. The position then taken was to review this with the price cap review in 1996/97, and this remains the position. Under the 1992 licence modifications BT now produces its regulated accounts on both a CCA and an HCA basis for OFTEL.

Current Pricing Régime

Having discussed some economic theory, I will now examine the current régime. The current system of interconnection pricing involves the use of fully allocated costs (on an historic basis), augmented by access deficit contributions (ADCs). The fully allocated cost mechanism for establishing interconnection charges is broadly equivalent to an equal mark-up on direct or incremental costs for all interconnection services charged to all customers (including BT Retail). Implicitly, the mark-up over costs is applied to both wholesale and retail services. There is no evidence that this is, even approximately, an efficient way of recovering common costs, nor that it replicates the outcome of a competitive or contestable market in interconnection services. A further disadvantage of current arrangements is that costs are computed in a backward-looking way, based upon historic cost accounts.

The current system of access deficit contributions also has interesting features. If we view the access deficit as an overhead which has to be borne by various components of usage (local, national and international), then the question arises as to how to share it out. One possibility would be to distribute it in accordance with call minutes; under a second, it could be distributed in accordance with direct costs. In fact, the sharing rule is based upon the profitability of the relevant call. The justification is that entrants concentrating their activities in profitable markets should find a reflection of their behaviour in their access deficit contribution. The ADC system can thus be viewed as a bowdlerised version of the

ECPR, which requires interconnecting operators to compensate the incumbent for the profit it forgoes as a result of their entry. Certainly, the current arrangements are some way from providing an economically efficient set of prices and this concern is a major factor behind the present review.

Summary

Pulling these points together, we can say that the outcome for interconnection is closely dependent on the extent of tariff rebalancing in final services markets. To meet the objectives of economically efficient and sustainable competition, interconnection charges need to be linked in some way to final prices. In a world of unbalanced tariffs there are grounds for suggesting an ECPR approach but modified to take account of any inefficiency on the part of the incumbent, with some facility available to allow for the entry costs associated with new operators. Alternatively, in a rebalanced world, something like the Ramsey approach may be more appropriate, with charges differentiated by the nature of final services provided and, typically, involving a mark-up over incremental costs. These mark-ups could be adjusted to reflect efficiency and other objectives of regulation.

However, the complexities of establishing the demand characteristics required for this régime should not be underestimated. Current thinking is a long way from conclusion, though it is clear that any revised interconnection arrangement will need to take explicit account of the costs of social provision and how such costs might best be recovered.

The Way Forward

As already mentioned, OFTEL is addressing all of these issues. It is too early to say what conclusions will be reached. However, it does seem likely that some alteration to the present régime will result. Although the régime is workable it is seen as confusing, opaque and uncertain and thus hardly conducive to delivering the higher degree of customer service and choice expected when the market was liberalised in 1991.

The aim of the current review is to establish a transparent, robust and durable system of interconnection. It is crucial that we get it right. In seeking to do so, a full appreciation of the opportunities and problems facing new entrants is essential. I have spoken about the unbalanced nature of tariffs and the attraction this presents for entry, but equally, new entrants face the challenges of competing against new and emerging technologies and some entrants have substantial coverage obligations to meet. In some cases the choices and opportunities facing new entrants are less than those facing the incumbent. The issue is to what extent and in what ways should this impact on the interconnection régime.

Perhaps I could finish by setting out two further aspects of OFTEL policy objectives that will underpin the current review of interconnection.

As I mentioned earlier, the arrangements to date have tended to favour the development of infrastructure competition. In the main only operators offering network facilities are able to obtain cost-based interconnection. Other operators are faced with purchasing facilities at a retail tariff. The question is whether this should continue to be the case if the objectives are to provide customers with a level of services equal to the best in the world. There is a tension here. Allowing non-network service suppliers access to cost-based interconnection could provide a disincentive to the development of competing networks. An additional problem is that it could undermine the existing price cap on BT's retail services, especially if competition with BT's retail services becomes intense. Quite how this issue will be resolved is unclear but it looks as though price will, as always, play a key rôle.

A further policy objective for consideration is the extent to which service innovation might best be encouraged. Clearly, innovation is a critical component of the provision of a high-quality service for the customer, but how should interconnection charges be set to ensure that this is achieved? A policy designed to ensure one operator's new services are immediately made available to all other operators, at cost, might produce the wrong incentives to innovative development, though it may have short-term attractions for customers of such services.

Efficiency, choice, competition and innovation are some of the key objectives OFTEL is looking at very closely at present. I am grateful for the opportunity to raise them here.

DISCUSSANT'S COMMENTS

John Kay
Visiting Professor of Economics, London Business School

ALAN BELL HAS GIVEN US A COMPREHENSIVE OVERVIEW of the theory and issues in relation to interconnect pricing. But what concerns me is that it is very little different from the paper he or other people would have given on the theory and practice of interconnect pricing 10 years ago. Since then we have been debating these issues. I suspect that the conclusion which will come out of the current round of discussions will once again be that we need over the next few years to develop thinking about all this further. In the meantime, what we will do is to go on relying on further development of British Telecom's accounting systems, based on financial results by services.

No Progress – Are Economists at Fault?

I do not want at all to blame Oftel for that; I do not think it is Oftel's responsibility. What I do want to do is to ask why we are not making further progress? I suggest that a lot of the blame for that falls at the door of economists. In some ways we are pursuing the wrong accounting theory.

I talked about some broader issues and network pricing in this lecture series last year.[1] The key point there, from my perspective, relates to a point which Alan Bell raised. He said that ideally one would base interconnect prices on incremental costs, but the problem was that incremental costs differed from average costs where there were economies of scale and scope.

Now there are quite a number of reasons why average and incremental costs differ. Average and incremental costs would always be the same if, *first*, there were no economies of scale and scope; *second*, capacity everywhere in the system was at its optimum level; *third*, historic and current costs were the same; *fourth*, there were no inefficiency relative to current best practice anywhere in the system; and *fifth*, there were no 'inclusional' or 'exclusional' errors, about which I will say more in a

---

[1] John Kay, 'Regulating Networks', in Michael Beesley (ed.), *Regulating Utilities: The Way Forward*, IEA Readings No.41, London: Institute of Economic Affairs, 1994.

moment. But if all of these conditions were fulfilled, there would simply be no difficulty in reconciling analysis based on average costs with analysis based on incremental costs. The reason there are difficulties in practice is because of those factors.

In my experience, by far the most important of these is the fifth – errors of inclusion versus errors of exclusion. When people calculate incremental cost, they leave too many things out, and when they calculate average cost, they put too many things in. When you start to consider what really needs to be included in incremental cost, what is in average cost, and then what is actually relevant to the provision of that particular service, you discover that the apparent gaps between incremental and average cost, which are typically asserted to be enormous, turn out to be much narrower than you think. Even in my own business it is a constant battle to persuade people that, if anything, we run a business that is characterised by dis-economies of scale. Marginal costs are not below average costs; they are above them.

But if we disregard inclusion and exclusion for the moment, and assume we have measured incremental costs and average costs correctly, then it is not the first that is primarily responsible for the difference; it is the second, third and fourth, namely, the existence of capacity shortages and surpluses, the differences between historic and current cost, and the existence of historic inefficiency versus assumed best practice.

Not only that, if it were not true that the second, third and fourth of these factors are far more important than the first, the whole policy of promoting competition and interconnect in this and other industries would be misconceived. Because if it really were just the first that was at issue – that the dominating element was economies of scale and scope – the right answer in all of these industries would simply be to have a single firm, the incumbent. In that case, one would set interconnect prices at levels at which there would in practice be no interconnect, and no entry. The reason it makes sense to have interconnect, or the reason government has adopted this kind of policy, is that it leaves two, three and four, and particularly four, as more important than one – as indeed they are in most areas we are looking at (in particular in telecoms). Competition is now emerging in all areas of the business, a pretty clear indication that it is not economies of scale and scope which are the critical element in all of this, but rather two, three and four.

Pursuing the Wrong Theory?

I said we were pursuing the wrong economic theory. As Alan described them, the theories, largely developed in the United States to deal with particular issues of efficient component pricing and of Ramsey rules, are predicated on the assumption that the problems we have to deal with are those arising from economies of scale and scope. If we reject that assumption, we have to deal with the other factors in a rather different way.

First, as far as capacity shortages and surpluses are concerned, the issue is whether a regulator wishes charges to be set by reference to short-run or long-run incremental cost. The answer depends on the time-horizons in relation to the particular business and whether he is more concerned to attract short-term efficient use of the system, or whether he is concerned to give the right signals for long-run planning. This has nothing to do with 'efficient component' pricing.

Second, there is the problem of differences between historic and current cost, and there the position is absolutely clear. Historic cost is entirely irrelevant to appropriate levels of interconnect pricing; what matters are current costs. The third issue is historic inefficiency versus assumed best practice. How should a regulator set interconnect prices, when he knows costs could be lower than they are? The answer depends on whether his primary objective is to promote more efficiency on the part of the incumbent, in which case he will set prices closer to best practice than to historic levels, or whether his primary concern is to attract new, more efficient entrants into the industry, in which case he will be content to allow prices to remain at historic levels, knowing they are likely to be undercut by the provision of new facilities.

Developing Accounting Theory

You will notice that in none of these cases have I mentioned Ramsey rules or efficient component pricing. They are simply not relevant to the issue at hand. We ought really to be pursuing some accounting theory rather than some economic theory. Developing accounting theory turns out to be very helpful in pursuing these issues. Even if the economic theory of this has not advanced a lot in the last 10 years, the accounting theory has.

Ten years ago there were two main accounting propositions, which were inconsistent. One was the idea that you can mostly attribute joint costs only if you employ enough engineers to look very closely at the production processes. And the second fallacy was that all joint cost allocations are arbitrary. You will find them still in all but the most modern of management accounting textbooks. But we have learnt better in the last few years, from two main sources, namely, activity-based costing and attribution by reference to commercial purpose, and from the fact that allocations of joint costs are not in the main arbitrary. One may attribute quite a lot, in many cases the whole, of joint costs to particular purposes by adopting essentially a game theoretic approach to understanding what is going on. The second part of the theory has been largely developed by economists and the first part by accountants.

It is said that practical men are the slaves of some defunct economist. I fear that may be the case in interconnect, and is the reason why we are not making faster progress.

4

DEVELOPING COMPETITION: REGULATORY INITIATIVES

Clare Spottiswoode
Ofgas

Introduction

THE UK GAS MARKET IS truly in transition. The previously integrated industry is being restructured and re-regulated to promote competition over all of supply and more of the transmission system. We appear to have support from all the major players.

British Gas wants competition. On 8 September 1994, Cedric Brown, Managing Director of British Gas (BG), was quoted in the *London Evening Standard* as urging ministers to 'get on with it' and free up the market as soon as possible and to 'stop delaying and put an end to uncertainty'.

Consumer groups say they want competition. Jim Cooper, the Chairman of the Gas Consumers' Council (GCC) has said: 'It is high time that the Government ended uncertainty and gave competition the fair wind it deserves.' Dr John Beishon, Chief Executive of The Consumers' Association, has written to the President of the Board of Trade saying he supports competition as early as possible. He told Mr Heseltine: 'We share your view that a truly competitive market, offering consumers a genuine choice of gas supplier, is the best spur to quality improvement and lower prices.'

At the time of the 1994 Labour Party Conference, Labour's front bench energy spokesman, Martin O'Neill, went out of his way to emphasise that the Labour Party had no interest or intention of seeking to return British Gas to the public sector. And he added: 'It is not the function of Labour to defend British Gas as the monopoly supplier of gas to any sector of the UK gas market.' He went on to urge the Government to include a Gas Bill in the forthcoming Queen's Speech. So Labour is in favour of competition. The independent suppliers, of course, do not need convincing. They are keen to move to full competition as soon as possible.

Much of this new impetus stems, of course, from the MMC Gas Reports of 1993, and subsequent developments. After a period of public consultation on the MMC reports, the Secretary of State announced his decision in December 1993.[1] *First*, BG was to separate its transportation and storage and trading businesses but not by divesting the trading arm as MMC had recommended. Instead, he believed the complete separation of the businesses within BG ownership, if vigilantly pursued and monitored, would be sufficient to overcome the obstacle to competition which the MMC had identified.

Second, he announced the intention to open the market to competition below 2,500 therms in stages from April 1996, with full competition from April 1998. From these events have sprung many of the initiatives presently under way.

The restructuring of a previously integrated industry to promote competition is a complex task which cannot be achieved overnight. But considerable progress has already been made. There are essentially three parts to this:

- separation;

- a Network Code;

- full competition in supply.

I will cover the last first. Before doing so I should point out that we need proper separation and a Network Code to cope with the competition that exists already. If a customer uses more than 2,500 therms a year – about four times the average domestic consumption – he can already buy gas from essentially unregulated companies.

Opening the Domestic Market to Competition

When I use the word 'domestic', I am talking about the market below 2,500 therms. We are currently making no distinction between domestic and small industrial and commercial customers. A joint OFGAS/DTI consultation document on how to introduce competition was published in May 1994.[2] We had a deluge of responses – from consumers, large and small, interest groups, and of course the industry. The formal reply from BG was considerably longer than the consultation document itself! Consultation and discussion are still going on. We are now reasonably

---

1 Department of Trade and Industry, Press Release P93/759: 'Heseltine announces decision on MMC report on gas industry', 21 December 1993.

2 *Competition and choice in the gas market: a joint consultation document*, OFGAS/DTI, May 1994.

hopeful of getting legislation. If we get it, all these views will be debated in Parliament.

Matters are, therefore, by no means finally settled, especially as to the finer details, but some of the main aspects of the proposals as they presently stand are as follows. *First*, some principles:

- The structure must work even if there is no dominant player. We cannot expect another Gas Bill for many years.

- There must be a 'level playing field' with the only exceptions being for dominance.

- We need a pro-competitive structure with the ability to increase the scope for competition over time.

- There must be protection for consumers – but the protection given must also make regulatory and competitive sense.

1.   Transitional Arrangements

The intention is to open the market to competition in stages, beginning in April 1996, with full competition by April 1998. The precise transitional arrangements are still being formulated. At present, the thought is that competition will start in April 1996 in a pilot area of about 500,000 customers. This pilot is intended to ensure systems are in place to allow a smooth transfer of large numbers of customers from one supplier to another. In 1997, the pilot is expected to expand to cover about two million customers. This could be in one or possibly several areas of the country. It is most likely two areas will be selected.

2.   Safety

If there is one thing which everyone agrees on it is that safety must remain a priority as the gas supply market is fully opened to competition. It will be important that there are clear arrangements to ensure public safety. I personally do not see this as an issue. There are safety concerns now, and our proposals for competition should not add to these, but legislation will give us a chance to sort out some existing weaknesses. British Gas (TransCo) is expected to have responsibility for providing an initial contact point for the public for emergency services and for dealing with gas leaks from its system – wherever they occur – whether outside in the street or within the home. The Health and Safety Commission is preparing a full assessment of the safety implications of a fully competitive market. The Commission's report was completed in late 1994.[3]

3. Security of Supply

This will be underwritten by a number of requirements including:

- A Network Code which will ensure an overall supply/demand balance.

- An obligation to supply all on published tariffs – at least initially.

- A requirement to maintain continuity of supply to existing customers.

- Arrangements in the event of commercial failure.

I will return to the Network Code below (p.59).

4. Pricing

Competition will encourage companies to seek the most cost-effective way of serving customers, and while it is not possible to forecast accurately the price benefits, independent gas suppliers say they expect to undercut British Gas's present prices. The commercial sector already enjoys price reductions of up to 20 per cent now that it is open to competition.

Independents have lower overheads, lower costs of service and billing, and we expect cost reductions as competing suppliers strive to buy gas at the keenest possible prices. In the long term, we should see improved efficiency in some of the supporting services as well, such as storage and metering, which at present are provided by British Gas; and more effective use of the network as companies respond to pricing signals. Services will be progressively unbundled, eventually leaving only the network as the regulated natural monopoly. On this basis, OFGAS considers that almost 30 per cent of the costs presently recovered through the transportation price control could eventually be subject to competitive pressures. These arrangements will be underpinned by:

- Published tariffs – unregulated;

- A regulated 'standby price' and deposit;

- A tariff formula while appropriate.

---

[3] Health and Safety Commission, *Britain's gas supply: a safety framework*, Health and Safety Executive, 1994.

5. Standards of Service

British Gas works to strict standards of service including debt and disconnection procedures, and has special arrangements for older and disabled people. These cost money to maintain and in a competitive market some customers may be willing to pay more for higher standards or by contrast accept lower standards in return for lower prices. We are considering whether British Gas Public Gas Supply should continue to be required to offer the present standards of service and to what extent obligations should be imposed on other suppliers. The aim here is not to raise the costs of entry unnecessarily, nor to insist on some gold-plated standards which customers, if free to choose, would not want.

Regulation of British Gas's Network

The objective of regulating British Gas's pipeline network is to provide truly open and equal access to all users of BG's network. Companies are not going to enter or stay in the market if they think barriers exist or are likely to emerge from BG's ownership of the main transportation and storage system. This calls for effective separation between BG's transportation and storage business and its trading businesses.

Separation has many facets. Some of the more important ones are:

- The establishment of a separate price control over BG's Network.

- The establishment of a structure of charges for using the network which is applicable to all users of the system, including BG's own trading businesses.

- Clear organisational and informational separation between BG's transportation and storage business and its trading businesses.

Price Control

The 1993 MMC report required OFGAS to put in place a price control for transportation and storage separate from that for the tariff market. The new price control took effect from 1 October 1994. Its main features are:

- the form of the control is RPI-X, as recommended by the MMC;

- X has been set at 5, in line with the rates of return recommended by the MMC;

- the control will last until April 1997; and

- the control covers transportation and storage together, with a provision requiring British Gas not to cross-subsidise unduly between its transportation and storage activities. Separating the two is a complex task, and will be taken forward in the next price control review.

Work on a new price control, which will take effect from 1 April 1997, will be starting soon. We will need to be in a position to make proposals to British Gas by the Summer of 1996. We issued a consultation document on the new price controls in May 1995.[4]

Structure of Charges

It was a recommendation of the MMC that a suitable structure of charges (or pricing methodology) should be established, endorsed by OFGAS, which would be applicable to all users of British Gas's transmission system, including BG's own trading businesses. OFGAS consulted on the structure of charges before Christmas 1993. In May 1994, British Gas made proposals for the year 1994/95. A new structure of charges was published in September, which took effect from 1 October 1994.

One feature which has attracted particular attention is that the charges for use of the national transmission system incorporate some regional differentiation. If charged out to domestic customers this would amount to ±2 per cent across the country. British Gas has always charged competitors distance-related charges for use of its system. And of course British Gas itself used to charge customers somewhat different prices in different regions until 1989. British Gas will be keeping its pricing methodology under review. And OFGAS will be reconsidering the structure of charges in the context of the 1997 price control review.

Separation

Our new decision document[5] is intended to ensure separation so that all parties have open and equal access to British Gas's transmission system. BG Transco will treat BG Trading at arm's length, like any other supplier or shipper. This is one of the more important prerequisites for effective competition in gas supply.

---

[4] *Price control review: British Gas' transportation and storage: a consultation document*, Ofgas, May 1995.

[5] *Separation of British Gas' transportation and storage business from its trading businesses: the Director General's decision*, Ofgas, February 1995.

We are already a long way down the road to effective separation. In December 1993 British Gas announced that it was restructuring the gas supply business to convert the existing structure of 12 regions in which transportation, storage and trading were closely integrated, into five separate national businesses – Transportation and Storage (TransCo), Public Gas Supply, Contract Trading, Retailing, and Servicing and Installation. It also introduced a temporary sixth unit to provide support services on a transitional basis for two years. This re-organisation has simplified the task of establishing organisational and informational separation of TransCo from British Gas's trading businesses.

But there are issues still to be considered which were raised in the consultation document we published in October 1994.[6] These include:

- the extent to which TransCo's management should have autonomy over its resources within British Gas's corporate structure;

- whether the arrangements put in place are likely to provide truly effective 'Chinese walls'; and

- whether there is a case for some services to be provided centrally by British Gas to TransCo, provided there are safeguards in place to protect the 'Chinese walls'.

We would very much welcome views on these and the other issues set out in our consultation document.

Network Code

Briefly, we intend to get a Network Code in place by October 1995. This will set out the rules to ensure that physical supply and demand are in balance across the national system. But it also covers many other areas, including, for example, the aspects covered in the electricity Grid Code, as well as some of the elements which are more like those dealt with in the electricity pool. It is an immense task which OFGAS is chairing with full participation of all interested parties. It is an uncomfortable rôle for a regulator and puts us in the firing line. However, without it I do not think we could possibly achieve a Network Code in the time available. Naturally there is controversy, and naturally there are compromises – but it does look as if we will succeed in establishing a Network Code by October 1995.

---

6 *Separation of British Gas' transportation and storage business from its trading businesses: a consultation document*, Ofgas, October 1994.

Conclusion

What of the future? The task of restructuring and re-regulating the previously integrated gas industry in a way that truly promotes competition is complex and will take some time to complete. It throws up challenges – not least for the Regulator. Our task is twofold.

First is the efficient regulation of a natural monopoly associated with the transportation of gas in a way that provides open and equal access to the system at reasonable prices. This amounts to pro-competitive regulation of the natural monopoly. It entails not only identifying what has to be done but also ensuring that it is done.

Second, we are seeking ways of introducing competition into services which have been traditionally monopolised. Opening the whole of the gas supply market to competition is clearly one of the most important tasks here. And again, pro-competitive regulation entails not only identifying what needs to be done, but ensuring that it happens.

In the next few years the Regulator is likely to be busier than ever. There will, for example, be the resetting of the price controls over British Gas's transmission system to take effect from April 1997. And there is much more to be done to ensure competition is firmly established in the supply of gas to all customers. This is a difficult task. For OFGAS to do its job properly we clearly have to take account of the concerns and opinions of those affected by our decisions. We also need to tap into the expertise within the gas industry and amongst those who study the industry and represent consumers.

This calls for open and inter-active regulation, not only to address concerns about the accountability of regulators, but to help ensure we perform our tasks in the best possible way. In general, our aim is clear: to help promote competition where it is possible and only to substitute regulation where it is essential. We need all the help we can get to undertake that task effectively.

DISCUSSANT'S COMMENTS

Geoffrey Whittington
Price Waterhouse Professor of Financial Accountancy,
University of Cambridge

Introduction

I SHARE WITH THE DIRECTOR-GENERAL two assumptions: first, that competition is the most desirable means of regulation, and, second, that regulatory intervention may be necessary to foster and preserve competition, especially in the presence of a natural monopoly, such as is held by British Gas in transmission and distribution.

Having agreed on fundamental objectives, I am sceptical about the introductory comments which suggest universal enthusiasm for 'competition'. When parties as diverse as British Gas, the independent suppliers, the GCC, the Consumers' Association, the Government, and the Labour Party are all apparently agreed, this suggests contradictory views as to what is meant by 'competition' or its practical manifestations. For example, the independent suppliers would no doubt hope for the right to 'cherry pick' the market in 'competition' with a British Gas which had one, and preferably both, its hands tied behind its back by regulations. British Gas, on the other hand, is no doubt keen to end uncertainty and on removing some regulatory constraints to 'free up the market', and much less keen on measures which encourage independent suppliers. The Regulator has to balance such competing interests, and will find it impossible to please all parties at the same time. Hence, the vision of harmony may be wishful thinking.

Scepticism turns almost into cynicism when we are told by the Regulator that 'much of this new impetus stems, of course, from the MMC Gas Reports of 1993...' (above, p.53).

Divestment, Not 'Chinese Walls'

The MMC's main proposed remedy (dubbed aptly by our Legal Adviser as 'The Great Remedy') was the total separation of British Gas's trading interests from its transportation interests, by means of divestment. The MMC believed that this was an essential precondition for healthy, self-sustaining competition in the gas trading market. Lesser separation by means of 'Chinese Walls' upon which the Regulator is now working was rejected by the MMC for good reasons, including the cost and unreliability of such arrangements and the fact that only divestment could remove the potentially perverse incentives resulting from common ownership (for example, higher transportation charges are a real cost to independent shippers, but not to British Gas Trading when looked at in the context of the Group as a whole). If the separation by Chinese Walls *is* successful, what advantages does it confer that could not be achieved by the simpler and more foolproof process of divestment? In particular, why did OFGAS, which now has a continuing problem of policing the Chinese Walls, support the Secretary of State's decision?

The most important subsidiary recommendation by the MMC was the phased abolition of the tariff monopoly. However, this was a *recommendation*, not a *remedy*, because the MMC did not make an adverse finding on the working of the tariff market. In other words, the tariff market was working fairly well, so orderly improvement was more important than drastic remedies (which we were not, in any case, permitted to propose in the absence of an adverse finding). Moreover, the total reform, which we recommended to come into force by the year 2002, would be a liberalised gas market which would be unique in the world, no other country having achieved completely free access by competitive suppliers over a gas distribution network owned by a third party. In view of the experimental nature of this system and the security problems of gas supply, we felt that the 'big bang' approach had an ominous ring to it in this particular industry!

Thus, the policy which OFGAS is currently implementing is not that of the MMC but that of the Government: it should be noted that the Government's policy of phasing out the tariff monopoly pre-dates the MMC references and has not changed since the Reports of the MMC.

The Director-General's paper describes the progress which has been made in implementing this policy in accordance with the timetable set by the Secretary of State in consultation with OFGAS. As a sceptical member of the MMC group, I wonder if this timetable is realistic. The problem of finding parliamentary time for the new Gas Bill may lead to its collapse at the first hurdle. This might provide a welcome respite for those whose task it is to develop the new system!

Nevertheless, OFGAS is now committed to these policies, and, as the paper reports, has taken some steps towards achieving them.

Opening the Below-2,500 Therm Market to Competition

It is, correctly, proposed that 'the licensing régime will put certain obligations on all suppliers'. There are two difficulties with this requirement: Will the obligations be appropriate, and can they be enforced?

Here the main anxieties must be 'cherry picking' and 'free riding' by independent suppliers. 'Cherry picking' is acknowledged implicitly as a problem and some obvious measures are suggested, such as an obligation to supply on a first-come first-served basis, but there are loopholes such as the choice of area of operation, the let-out when the limit of supply is reached, marketing policy, and pricing policy. It should not be difficult to price 'undesirables' out of the market, or simply to fail to inform them of the availability of independent suppliers. British Gas, or large independents, may be required to pick up this business, but at a price. This is, of course, what is implied by full rebalancing, but the social and political consequences may be unacceptable. From British Gas's point of view, there is a disturbing degree of ambivalence about when it is to be relieved of onerous obligations and allowed to compete on equal terms – for example, the Director General talks of removal of British Gas's statutory monopoly, but not of its statutory obligations.

The possibility of free-riding arises from the mutual insurance schemes to cover failure by a shipper: if this is avoided by insisting on individual insurance, small shippers will no doubt claim that the cost is an unfair barrier to entry. There is also a potentially serious free-rider problem if metering is not comprehensive: shippers supply to and draw from a common pool and the cost of gas depends not only on location and volume but also on time of year. There are 18 million customers in the tariff market, so a great deal of monitoring will be required.

All these problems will, no doubt, be resolved by a process of experiment, but it will take time. Hence my scepticism about the *timetable*. One good feature of the timetable is, however, the proposal to conduct the initial experiments comprehensively within specified geographical areas. This will enable the new system to be tested on a full cross-selection of customers, rather than a nationally 'cherry-picked' élite.

Regulation of British Gas's Network

The *price control* to transportation and storage does substantially follow the MMC's recommended structure, and the level seems to have been set in a suitably 'firm but fair manner'. British Gas's initial complaints and subsequent acceptance of the new control are consistent with this view. One reservation is that transportation and storage charges will not be separated by regulation until the next price review (to take effect in 1997). One of the benefits of freeing the tariff market should be that the demand for storage and interruptibility should be no longer a monopsony of British Gas. Potential players in this new market might benefit from an early warning about future storage charges by British Gas.

The *organisational and informational separation* has already been referred to. In my view, this is making the best of a bad job, and in some respects not even that: full financial autonomy for TransCo, with no centrally-provided services, seems to be desirable. Any allowance of centrally-provided services should be supported by compelling evidence as to the associated economies of scope or scale, and the purchase of and payment for such services should be on an arm's length commercial basis.

Conclusion

It is certainly likely that 'In the next few years the Regulator is likely to be busier than ever' (above, p.60) and that the establishment of greater competition will be 'a difficult task'. It is also an important one, and I hope that the Regulator demonstrates by practical achievement that the MMC's chosen route was not the only one which could lead to ultimate success.

5

REGULATORY RELATIONSHIPS BETWEEN KEY PLAYERS IN THE RESTRUCTURED RAIL INDUSTRY

John Swift QC
Office of the Rail Regulator

1 January 1993 to 1 December 1993

Special Adviser and Regulator Designate

IN JANUARY 1993 ROGER SALMON AND I were appointed Special Advisers to the Secretary of State for Transport in the expectation that if the Railways Bill achieved Royal Assent and if the Act contained provisions for the appointment of a Rail Regulator and a Franchising Director, I would be appointed Regulator and he Franchising Director.

The Government remained confident throughout 1993 that the Bill would be enacted. But it was a controversial and complex Bill. As the Special Adviser and Rail Regulator Designate, I was in the position of advising the person who would appoint me as to the kind of structure for the new railways industry which would be consistent with the public interest, while the 'public interest' – the set of objectives within Section 4 of the Act – was itself being redefined through the Parliamentary process.

Early Identification of Regulatory Risk

What is now Section 4(5) of the Act – *a duty to take into account until 31 December 1996 any guidance issued to the Regulator by the Secretary of State –* was added to the Bill as a new clause shortly after I was appointed Regulator Designate. That was my introduction to the concept of regulatory risk. As a legal adviser to several of the 'privatised utilities' I had considered *regulatory risk* as some chance, a possibility or a probability, that conduct of a dominant firm might attract the attention of a regulator and might be considered unacceptable or contrary to the purpose of the legislation: in other words, the risk was that of the dominant firm or regulated undertaking. And *regulatory capture* was the means by which regulatory risk would be eliminated.

There was, of course, another element of regulatory risk: that the Regulator might, by what he said and did in the exercise of his statutory powers, put at risk the achievement of the legitimate objectives of regulated firms and, more ominously, the Government's own objective in securing the *privatisation* of railway assets and undertakings and the *reconstruction* of the industry according to the plans of the Government, as shareholder, underwriter and ultimate controller of the railway businesses.

The Compromise

The Government had certain options. It could have left 'Section 4' as first drafted. It was based on the precedents of the Telecommunications Act 1984, the Gas Act 1986, the Electricity Act 1986, and the Water Act 1989. To permit the Government to 'guide' an independent regulator might *risk* the independence of the Regulator and thus hazard a principal object of the legislation. But not to amend might prejudice the privatisation of the assets. The conduct and performance in office of those appointed as Regulators, however estimable in the pursuit of the public interest, was seen as unpredictable. The 'Good Chaps' with the safe pairs of hands in Year 1 were believed to suffer some transformation into eccentric reconstructionists by Year 3, thereby injecting such a high degree of risk into a market sector as to raise the cost of entry or at worst impeding entry, competition and investment.

I did not know what my 'guidance' would be until I received it, almost a year later, on 31 March 1994. But by then much more had happened. I have referred to Section 4(5) for the obvious reason that it is unprecedented in earlier legislation and that it does constrain the 'independence' of the Regulator in a way different from other 'Section 4' duties. Looking back, could I or should I have objected to the inclusion of any such clause? I am satisfied that the time-limited guidance is reasonable. I am also satisfied that the concern as to regulatory risk was sufficiently serious that other ways could have and might then have been taken to reduce it during the period from the enactment of the Railways Act to the first substantial transfers of assets from the public sector to the private sector.

The Recognition by HMG of the Regulator's Independence

I can also say that throughout the period in which I was Special Adviser and Regulator Designate the Government, Ministers and Officials did not seek to change the *structure* of the Act so as to tilt the balance in their favour, or in favour of the Franchising Director, and against the Regulator. Sections 17-22 of the Act which confer upon the Regulator the power to direct the facility owners, including but not limited to Railtrack, to enter into access agreements on terms set by the Regulator – even while the facility owners are state-owned enterprises – remained in place as a critically important aspect of the new structure.

Early Statements on Independence and Regulatory Objectives

By the middle of 1993 I was, as it were, allowed out of Marsham Street to address a conference of senior managers of Regional Railways. What I said then I developed in speeches I gave in the conference season last winter, when the Bill had been passed. I have, I think, continued to adhere to the principles which I outlined then. They, in turn, are being further developed so as to form the Aim, Missions and Objectives of my Office, as follows:

- Independence

- Accountability

- Facilitating Reconstruction

- Control of Monopoly Abuse

- Consumer Protection

- Acting Fairly

So, in the first period, 1 January to 1 December 1993, I was involved in the transition from Bill to Act, in the process of the reconstruction, in the internal debates of Government and advised on future contractual relations. But the rôle was that of *adviser*. It could not be more. The decisions were those of the Secretary of State, responsible to Parliament.

1 December 1993 to 1 April 1994

The Appointment and Change in Status

On 1 December 1993, the then Secretary of State for Transport, Mr John MacGregor, appointed me as the Rail Regulator pursuant to Section 1 of the Railways Act 1993. But, with a few exceptions, none of the Regulator's statutory powers was brought into effect until 1 and 2 April 1994.

My team at 1 December consisted of about 10 people, including secretarial assistance. Slowly we began to build the structure of the new organisation. We knew that from April 1994 we might be called upon to exercise our powers, in respect of the approval of access agreements (Sections 17-22 of the Act), the enforcement of licences (Sections 55-57), closures (Sections 37-50), inquiries at the request of the new consumer committees and other matters, but it was impossible to predict how many new constituents would call.

The Vesting of the New Industry Undertakings

The period from 1 December 1993 to 1 April 1994 was one of intense activity. The Railways Act provided the statutory authority for the reconstruction – 'break up' is the expression of the dissenting movement – of the state-owned railway assets and businesses. By its commitment to transferring ownership and management of the infrastructure to Railtrack, a Government-owned company ('Go Co'), the Government was heavily reliant on the ability and determination of British Rail and Railtrack to secure the transfer by the vesting date of 31 March. But that was only part of the change. Twenty-five Train Operating Units (TOUs) had to be set up to manage British Rail passenger services operations as putative franchisees. Three Rolling Stock Leasing Companies (RSLCs) were created to own the locomotives and carriages. Three Freight Operating Companies (FOCs) took over the existing 'Train Load Freight' business of British Rail. British Rail Infrastructure Services, a division of British Rail, was to provide services of repair and renewal of infrastructure to Railtrack and to commence a process of reconstruction into 13 businesses to be transferred to the private sector in due course. Moreover, agreements had to be made as between Railtrack and British Rail, which both supplied services to and acquired services from each other.

Objectives but No Statutory Functions

Throughout that period until vesting my objectives were clear. I had no decision-making powers – but the arrangements to be put in place at vesting would be likely to continue so long as they met the commercial aspirations of the British Rail companies and Railtrack and the political aims of the Government and the Franchising Director. Even though I expected (but had no assurance) that my powers would be brought into existence immediately after vesting on 1 April, and that therefore I could change the elements of the 'contractual matrix' which required my consent, I had to participate in the development of the contractual matrix for three principal reasons.

First, to make it clear to the parties – by which I mean the Department of Transport, the Franchising Director, British Rail (including individual TOUs) and Railtrack – that if the contractual matrix in place for the beginning of the 1994/95 financial year was not, in the Regulator's view, compatible with the public interest they would know that and wish to avoid those consequences.

Second, that it was important to provide for a continuing rôle for the Regulator in the working out of the consequences of the new railway structure without substituting the Regulator for the old Command Structure of British Rail.

Third, that I would do what I could to ensure that the licences to be granted by the *Secretary of State* to Railtrack and to British Rail promoted the public interest objectives of the Act and provided an effective machinery for enforcement against abuse.

At the same time, the Government had several means by which it could control the *future* exercise by the Regulator of his statutory powers. *First* (and this would have been such a disregard of statements made in Parliament that it would surely have been dismissed as anything other than a legal possibility), the Government could have delayed the coming into force of Sections 17-22 of the Act (the Regulator's powers under the 'Access Provisions') until, say, 31 December 1996. *Second*, it could by the use of the General Authority to be granted to the Regulator by the Secretary of State, control what the Regulator could or could not include in licences to be granted by the Regulator. The Government has in effect deprived the Regulator of some of the standard forms of consumer protection normally conferred on regulators. *Third*, as stated, it had the exclusive statutory power over the grant of the first licences.

Fairish Outcome

We finished the vesting with an outcome with which I was reasonably content. We had had a significant influence over the Railtrack Licence and over the British Rail Licence. We had had a similar influence over the terms of the so-called 'Track Access Conditions' – those terms of Access Contracts which have to be the same for all parties at all times and which provide for future multilateral changes by facility owners and access beneficiaries. I had a concordat with the Secretary of State under which the principal vesting contract – the track access agreement between Railtrack and British Rail under which British Rail was granted permission to use Railtrack's track for a charge determined administratively by Railtrack and its shareholder – would be of short-term duration and would be replaced in the course of the financial year 1994/95 by access agreements for track, station and Light Maintenance Depots *approved* by the Regulator. Freight Access contracts would come up for approval on their expiry.

It was also clear at vesting that the process to change from a single command structure in British Rail (and decisions influenced by government policy on transport in general and railways in particular) to a new 'rule-based' system formed by contracts, including those *not* regulated by the Regulator, which would be *fair, reasonable, manageable* and *promote the public interest*, was just beginning. Vesting in substance, if not in form, was a continuous process.

1 April 1994 to November 1994

By 2 April we were 'open for business', and by that date we had recruited 32 staff. We had not issued any 'prospectus' as to the principles which would govern the decisions of the Regulator: we had repeated that we would pursue the public interest objectives of the Railways Act, but that was saying little more than that we would act within the four corners of our statutory duties, we would act reasonably taking account of the matters relevant to our decisions, and we would act fairly, emphasising in particular the desirability of setting out the Regulator's own objectives so as to give assurances to the existing and future railway undertakings as to their future prospects within a regulated environment.

I was now in a position to commit my Department to the achievement of the following objectives. They brought together in a coherent way the substantial and unordered list of statutory duties set out in Section 4 of the Act, the general common law duties of procedural propriety, the principles of good administration, the guidance of the Secretary of State (to be taken into account until 31 December 1996), the spirit of the legislation, and the rôle of the Regulator himself. In the absence of such analysis, and the elaboration of clear and binding principles, and the explanation of those principles to the 'constituents', decision-making would appear arbitrary, possibly unfair, leading to a lack of credibility in the process itself.

Simply to reiterate that the Regulator's primary function is to use his statutory powers to promote the public interest as an independent decision-maker, while important to state, does not seem to me sufficient to enable those expected to compete, to contract with each other, to invest for the future and to run their own businesses, to 'plan for the future'. Section 4(5) of the Act did not stand alone in seeking to manage regulatory risk. The Regulator's duty to enable operators to plan for the future with a reasonable degree of assurance and to impose minimum restrictions on operators consistent with the performance of his statutory duties was also consistent with going out of one's way to explain, to consult, to guide and to listen to the arguments of the new players.

In brief, the critical objective by which the Regulator will be judged within the next two or three years is:

- the right decisions,

- arrived at through fair processes,

- connected to each other through the promotion of the public interest within the right timetable.

The Right Decisions

What is the object or spirit of the Railways Act? Is it plain? Are there ambiguities? Is it appropriate to take the words of the statute and, as it were, order them where no order or set of priorities has been set by Parliament? The extensive powers conferred upon the Regulator have, of course, to be exercised to do justice in individual cases. But I see no danger in the articulation of governing principles. I express the principles, which must be pursued together, as follows:

- to secure the right balance of advantage among the new businesses within the rail industry so that each can plan for the future and invest in a better railway system;

- to promote and maintain competitive structures and competitive practices;

- to facilitate the process of restructuring the industry with an aim to its privatisation;

- to protect consumers from the possibility of market exploitation or market failure;

- to promote network benefits and the use of the railways generally.

The Right Balance of Advantage

One of the neologisms which has gained acceptance is the 'win-win situation'. No one could disagree with such a concept if it means that contracting interdependent undertakings settle terms and conditions (and prices) which provide incentives to improve the performance of each, to the benefit of both. It may involve the waiver of rights to pursue claims against the other contracting party; it will usually involve the payment of extra remuneration to reward exceptional performance. Fine, so long as the incentives are there to make the *dominant* partner even more efficient. So, where do we stand? Is it sensible or necessary for a regulator to intervene in the settling of contracts between mutually dependent undertakings?

Railtrack has a legal and a natural monopoly over the British domestic rail network. Its customers – the passenger train operators and the freight train operators – operate, to a greater or lesser degree, in competitive markets but they are dependent on Railtrack for their permission to use the infrastructure and for Railtrack's efficient performance of its responsibilities under their contracts and more generally.

Neither the identity of Railtrack's shareholder nor the existence of the Franchising Director as a surrogate buyer of Railtrack's capacity nor the competitiveness of some, but not all, of Railtrack's customers' markets should deflect the Regulator from pursuing, with efficiency, the standard objectives of the regulation of monopoly power – the 'stick' of prohibitions and the 'carrot' of retained profit attributable to 'Skill, industry and foresight'.

The prohibitions are those directed at the exploitation of monopoly (including inefficiency and refusal to supply) and at anti-competitive conduct, in particular in discriminating unfairly against users in the same market. This has particular relevance to the freight market.

I have set out in a consultation document issued in July the matters I think are relevant in a determination of the structure and level of Railtrack's charges for franchised passenger services. If prices are unfairly high they provide an inappropriate return to shareholders in relation to cost and risk and may reduce demand for services below an appropriate level. If the method of arriving at price is not transparent, users cannot adjust their own operations to make effective use of an essential service. And if prices in long-term agreements stay the same but efficiencies improve, the shareholder obtains a benefit at an unfair cost to the user. All this is fairly standard.

I am not proposing to debate those issues in this paper. In any event, it would be premature to announce my conclusions. In a lecture addressing the relationships between key players, I simply wanted to confirm the fact that under the Railways Act, Railtrack's future revenue streams in respect of the bulk of its business will be earned from contracts and that the Regulator, not the Government as shareholder and not the Government as the source of subsidy to the Franchising Director, determines the prices. That authority under the Act carries with it responsibilities to users of the network and to Railtrack to ensure that users are protected and also that the Regulator does not make it unduly difficult for Railtrack to finance its activities (particularly in relation to efficient investment).

I can say, however, that the quality and quantity of responses to the consultation paper has been high – including detailed comments from British Rail and from Railtrack, the two principal state-controlled undertakings. Each could have, politely but firmly, rejected the offer to respond and to engage in further detailed discussions and simply referred me to the terms of the guidance issued to me by the Secretary of State (annexed to my first Annual Report). The guidance to which I have referred above commends the adoption of the policy principles set by the Government as shareholder, including MEAV and the target of 8 per cent return on assets.

In brief, my belief is that Parliament has authorised me, even at this stage of reconstruction, to seek an objective justification for the level and structure of Railtrack's charges. I am delighted with the positive responses we have had. The issue is, of course, closely connected with the process of restructuring and the expected privatisation of Railtrack in due course.

Promoting Competition

The Regulator has a specific duty under the Act to promote competition. I wish that it were simple to reconcile the performance of that duty, in so far as it concerns competition *as between* passenger train operators, with other duties including the protection of users, the promotion of the network, the need to have regard to the financial position of the Franchising Director and my more general objective of facilitating entry of private finance and private sector initiatives into the railway industry.

Again, I have issued a consultation paper on this subject[1] and we are close to conclusions. Putting each side of the case at its most extreme, it is plain that I will have to arrive at a balance of advantage.

If 'open access' is denied, that is to say, if I place a restriction on Railtrack in all 25 relevant track access agreements that Railtrack will not grant any rights of access to a potential competitor on a line of route *and* I maintain that restriction in full force and effect for the period of the franchise, then the *only* competition which can take place will be between existing British Rail businesses using the track access rights conferred under their agreements with Railtrack. No one, apparently, is in favour of the ossification of the network but that would be a possible consequence.

But if 'open access' is granted, that is to say, if I place no restriction on

---

[1] *Competition for Railway Passenger Services: A Consultation Document*, ORR, July 1994.

Railtrack's ability to sell more of its capacity than is required by the 'incumbent' operator or operators, there is or may be scope for the cherry picker to take revenue and profit from the incumbent, reducing or eliminating the possibility of cross-subsidy as between different train 'diagrams'. In its most extreme form, the consequence might be the creation of such uncertainty that the market would be seen as unattractive for investment in incumbents or an acceleration of closures of services or price increases in inelastic markets to produce more revenues which the Franchising Director could tax.

For my part, the position is that the Franchising Director is to propose; our duty is to dispose, taking into account the guidance given by the Secretary of State that moderation of competition may be required in order to secure the transfer of passenger railway operators into the private sector.

Facilitate Process of Restructuring into Private Sector

There is no reference to 'privatisation' in the Regulator's Section 4 duties. But there is such a reference in the Secretary of State's 'Guidance' to the Regulator. And plainly it is a principal object of the legislation and the justification for a substantial 'conversion cost' from vertically integrated transport undertaking to inter-dependent trading companies.

The political, economic and social case for privatisation has been put, and contested, over several years. It would be wholly inappropriate for the Regulator to frustrate the objects of the legislation. At the same time, the other key players have to recognise that if they want regulatory approval for the contracts over which the Regulator has jurisdiction they must assist the Regulator in submitting agreements which are 'fit for purpose' – in this case the advancement of the public interest and the promotion of the separate objectives set out in Section 4 of the Act. At the risk of oversimplifying a complex project which should be completed by the end of 1994/95, our aim is to make 'the right decisions within the right timetable'.

In order to assist that process, we are setting out the criteria relevant to the approval of track access agreements for franchised passenger services. We are consulting on the broader issues of Railtrack's charges (including freight access charging) and competition. We have issued Guidance on Applications for Licensees to operate trains, stations and depots. And we are already investigating allegation of breach of licences so as to establish clear rules and an indication of our policies in respect of issues such as discrimination between competing train operators at stations.

We also have to exercise a degree of self-discipline in the process of 'regulation'. My objective is to let the contracts meet the aspirations of the parties as the first objective. A set of rights and obligations which is imposed by an external authority is no substitute for a commercially negotiated contract; and it may have the perverse and unwanted consequence of discouraging the acquisition of the assets or the undertaking itself. This has particular force where the Franchising Director has to 'sell' the regulated agreement or agreements.

We are in the early days of our decision-making, in respect of the 'regulated agreements'. We take account of representations made to us by the Franchising Director and by other key players. We have a common interest in taking decisions which will lead to a better railway system. But we also have to bear in mind that Railtrack, in a dominant position, is dealing with units within British Rail, the old state monopoly, according to a programme delivered by Government, according to the Government's timetable and executed by the Franchising Director acting according to instructions from the Government. It is important that we take the right decisions and have the time to take them within a timetable set for us and not by us.

Consumer Protection

The White Paper envisaged that the Regulator would be concerned with protecting the interests of those seeking access rights from facility owners and with the application, concurrently with the Director General of Fair Trading, of competition law in so far as it affected the interests of consumers. The Franchising Director and not the Regulator would be concerned in establishing minimum standards of consumer protection in respect of franchised passenger train operator services.

Thus, when the Government accepted a back-bench amendment to the Bill about control of fares it introduced the amendment in a form in which the 'duty to exercise a discretion' in respect of control of fares was imposed on the Franchising Director and not on the Regulator.

Similarly, when the Government issued a General Authority to the Regulator in respect of the Regulator's functions to grant licences the Regulator was expressly prohibited from imposing conditions on fares or the quality of services to be supplied to passengers on trains or on stations.

Why is this so? The Regulator has a statutory duty to *protect* users, which must include passengers, even though his only *express* duty to control fares concerns non-franchised suppliers of passenger train services who have a monopoly position – a *rara avis*. Indeed, the Regulator was referred to by Government Ministers, during the passage of the Bill through Parliament, as the protector of the consumer.

There are several reasons for conferring jurisdiction on the Franchising Director. *First*, the Franchising Director will have a contract with the passenger train operator under which the Franchising Director will be seeking value for money, and is himself under a duty to impose certain standards of performance. If that duty is being performed it would be administratively burdensome at least to have the Regulator exercising a separate sanction under the licence. *Second*, the Regulator is not a taxing authority. If fares do not cover the costs of providing the relevant services the Regulator would be placed in an impossible position, constitutionally, if he kept prices down at a cost to the taxpayer. *Third* (and this consideration applies with particular force to problems arising from unmanned stations), there should be more discretion left to the passenger train operators to make 'unregulated' decisions in 'unregulated' markets.

The Government policy to remove those elements of 'double jeopardy' does not touch, to their disadvantage, the User Committees. Indeed, they have a new remit to consider fares in addition to retaining the former statutory responsibilities for the protection of the interest of the passengers. Moreover, the Franchising Director must consult the Regulator before exercising his powers regarding fares control.

At this stage I can say that we would expect to be kept informed of policy decisions and their implementation in respect of train operators' duties to protect the consumers in the field of fares and quality of service. Our main functions in consumer protection are in areas where the train operators voluntarily or under the terms of their licences agree to supply services in combination with each other or provide services for the benefit of the network as a whole.

Network Benefits and the Use of the Railway

The Regulator has a specific duty to promote the use of the railway network; for the passenger, 'network benefits' mean that he should be entitled to travel on a *through ticket* from Penzance to Aberdeen, without concern that the Edinburgh-Aberdeen operator might challenge the validity of a ticket issued in Cornwall: it means that if train operator A's train is cancelled train operator B, using the same line of route, will not charge him again for a ticket issued by operator B (inter-availability); it also means that he can obtain information about the network and about services provided by train operators from a convenient source. But the passenger is now being offered something more: to 'train around'; to choose between the services of different train operators; to choose his combination of price and service.

This is an area in which there *has* to be *co-operation* in order to create the product or service without which passengers would cease to use the railway. Journeys which interconnect make a critically important contribution to industry revenues. I have no intention of requiring train operators to *refrain* from such co-operative activity, in the form of joint ventures voluntarily entered into or imposed by the Franchising Director, where the consumer benefits plainly outweigh the possible detriment of uncontrolled competition.

The Regulator and the Franchising Director are working together on these issues in a joint effort to arrive at licence conditions, enforceable by the Regulator, which will form part of the total set of obligations to be accepted by passenger train operators.

Concern has been expressed most forcefully by the General Secretary of the Rail, Maritime and Transport Union (RMT), that formation by the passenger train operators of a trade association – the Association of Train Operating Companies (ATOC) – would permit a 'cartel' to agree on all matters relating to passenger train services and the terms and conditions of employment. Such an agreement, it is alleged, would place the interests of the companies and their shareholders above those of their customers and their employees. I share some of Mr Knapp's concerns. We are all familiar with the morning and afternoon sessions of trade associations in which the morning is occupied with dull but virtuous matters such as the exchange of statistical information and reports by the technical committee whereas the afternoon, in the absence of Director Generals and competition lawyers, turns to more lively issues of collusion, predation and concealment.

But there is another side to the argument. Network benefits *cannot* be secured entirely by compulsion or *ad hoc* arrangements. At least at the beginning, it is in my view better to have a trade association, with an approved constitution, addressing issues which are of concern to passengers and operators. But ATOC must avoid the temptation of seeing itself as the collective body representing the interests of train operators against Railtrack. The relationship between Railtrack and its customers should be based on bilateral agreements approved by the Regulator with the machinery for future changes to the network and to the timetable settled in accordance with conditions, again approved by the Regulator, in which the relevant rights of the parties to initiate or oppose change are set out.

Summary

I have to avoid concentrating on a single issue or relying on a single formula to 'regulate' efficiently and fairly in the restructured railway industry. Even to put 'network benefits' at the top begs the question as to the size of the network. Moreover, I have to recognise that, for the foreseeable future, certainly for the period of tenure of my office, a substantial part of the network will remain in state ownership. Many if not all passenger train services will require subsidy and government will still undertake, on behalf of the general body of taxpayers, public service obligations as an alternative to line and station closures. It is not a simple market – and it is one in which government policies *and* the response by those invited to participate in the privatisation process will inevitably condition the policies of the Regulator.

At the same time, the Government, the Franchising Director, Railtrack and British Rail have an interest in knowing what the policies of the Regulator are. The most effective form of communication of policy is action or decision plus explanation. We are still in the early days of restructuring but I would express the relationship between the Regulator and the other key players as follows:

The Regulator and the Government

- Our policy is to facilitate the programme of privatisation within the timetable set by the Government.

- That means that in the regulatory process of approval of access agreements in the course of the current financial year we have to be vigilant and disciplined to ensure that we see the wood for the trees and manage commercial aspiration within a 'public interest' framework.

- We will monitor the performance of *all* the licensees, principally Railtrack and British Rail, irrespective of their ownership by the state, and we will take enforcement proceedings if necessary.

- We will take decisions on Railtrack's charges in the light of *all* our Section 4 duties including but not limited to taking account, until 31 December 1996, of the Secretary of State's guidance. In particular, we must be able to judge the *effect* on the market, including passengers and train operators, of any particular set of charges *proposed* by the dominant firm and its shareholder.

- We must ensure that the purposes and objects of the Act are not forgotten. The aim of the Act is *not* to replicate the entire British Rail organisation by a complex jigsaw puzzle which, when finally completed, looks the same as the original. The aim is to secure benefits to users and consumers through leaving *as much as possible* to the new key commercial players to determine. Government as shareholder and controller must be prepared to leave decisions to the market and to rely on the Regulator in the exercise of his independent function to act as the arbiter between those players in matters of dispute.

The Relationship with the Franchising Director

- We have a common interest in exercising our respective functions for the benefit of users and passengers.

- The Regulator accepts that the design of franchises, and the minimum standard specification imposed by the Franchising Director, are matters for the exercise of his discretion: the Franchising Director should accept that the Regulator has an independent duty to promote competition, as well as a duty to take into account guidance that competition may have to be moderated to assist the Franchising Director in 'selling' the businesses.

- The Franchising Director and Regulator have a common interest in securing access agreements which are fair and reasonable.

- The Franchising Director and Regulator have a common interest in agreeing the 'conditions' to be imposed on licensees in respect of through ticketing and network benefits generally.

- The Regulator is to be consulted in respect of fares.

- The resources of User Committees are available to the Franchising Director and to the Regulator.

DISCUSSANT'S COMMENTS

Ian Jones
National Economic Research Associates

JOHN SWIFT HAS GIVEN an extremely interesting account of the very distinctive characteristics of the new regulatory régime for railways, which reflect the underlying economic complexities of the industry within which regulation is being implemented. As discussant, I would like to focus on some of the issues John has raised in the two Consultation Documents the Office of the Rail Regulator (ORR) has issued, dealing respectively with on-rail competition and track access charges.

I begin by discussing some broad options for railway restructuring and privatisation. Given the economic and technical characteristics of the UK passenger railway, there are two viable alternative general models for industry restructuring and privatisation. I refer to these as, on the one hand, the Swedish, and, on the other, the Argentinian model.

The Swedish Model (Marginal Cost Basis)

The principal characteristics of the former are twofold: *first*, it involves the separation of infrastructure ownership and operation from the ownership and operation of mobile assets. *Second*, train operating companies pay fees to use infrastructure based on the marginal costs of infrastructure provision. I should add that in Sweden, train operators also pay the equivalent of vehicle excise duty at a fixed rate per vehicle, the intention being to create a charges régime that mirrors the road vehicle taxation arrangements and hence to equalise competition between those two modes of transport.

The technical characteristics of railways, in particular the very strong scale economies which exist in providing rail infrastructure services, probably extending to traffic levels beyond even those observed on the densest part of the British Rail network, mean that the revenues thus raised fall short of the full costs of infrastructure provision. As a consequence, the infrastructure owner receives a deficit grant from government, and, in Sweden, remains a public sector agency. Given marginal cost-based infrastructure charges, there is a core of profitable passenger services which can be competitively provided by the private sector. Unprofitable or 'social' railway services are provided through a set of exclusive franchise service agreements.

The Argentinian Model (Vertically Integrated)

The Argentinian alternative is quite different. The rail network is divided geographically by line of route into a series of vertically integrated exclusive franchise units. In this model, subsidy is injected through the franchise competition mechanism.

Each of these approaches has distinctive virtues and drawbacks. The Swedish approach emphasises allocative efficiency by ensuring that the major upstream input to rail service provision is supplied at marginal cost. It also addresses some of the problems of inter-modal competition between road and rail. It permits, and indeed encourages, competition between private sector train operating companies if demand is sufficiently intensive.

The principal disadvantage of this approach compared with the vertically integrated model is that the subsidy needed to provide a given level of final output of train services would be higher. The Argentinian approach, on the other hand, scores highly on encouraging cost-efficient provision of service through the periodic franchising competition process. By restricting on-rail competition it makes the surpluses above the marginal cost of infrastructure available to offset joint and common costs and so minimises subsidy. By retaining a vertically integrated structure, it avoids the cost burden of internalising externalities by contract mechanisms, and by maximising the value added directly controlled by franchisees, it brings competitive pressures to bear throughout the value chain.

Railways Act Framework – 'An Uncomfortable Marriage'

Now the framework created by the Railways Act, and subsequent ministerial directions or guidelines in the UK, represents, I believe, an uncomfortable marriage of the two approaches, and generates many of the difficulties in trying to regulate this new structure which John Swift has alluded to. Briefly, the key features of the arrangements are, *first*, that infrastructure ownership and operation are separated from train operation, with infrastructure assets vested in Railtrack. *Second*, passenger rail services are supplied primarily through a franchising process. However, the franchises are non-exclusive, so that franchisees face potential open-access competition from open-access operators who may, of course, be other franchisees.

The *third* characteristic is that both franchisees and open-access operators will pay track access charges to Railtrack. Now although open-access operators may gain access under the existing proposals the Government has put forward, as long as they are willing to pay more than the short-term variable costs incurred, Railtrack's charges will be set to recover its *full* costs, including eventually an 8 per cent real return on the full modern equivalent asset value of its plant. The bulk of railway track costs will in fact be recovered through a set of standing charges levied on each franchisee.

Fourth, subsidy will be injected through the franchising process. Franchise bids will therefore be based on the difference between expected passenger revenues and total costs including Railtrack's access charges.

The final ingredient in the mixture is that the Government has stated that Railtrack is to be privatised. This hybrid approach sets up a tension (which John Swift has touched on) between the objectives of promoting on-rail competition and of containing subsidy through the franchising mechanism. The stronger the threat of competition from open-access services, the more negative will be the sum of franchise bids and the higher will be the overall subsidy bill.

Conflict Recognised in Minister's Guidance

This conflict has been recognised in the Minister's guidance given to the Regulator by the Secretary of State earlier in 1994. It talks of the need to moderate competition to ensure the successful launch of the first generation of franchises. Accordingly, the Regulator should not require or approve access agreements that may prejudice or significantly interfere with the Franchising Director's programme. All this is to be done within the principles of access charging structure established for 1994/95.

Unfortunately, the track access charging structure referred to is very likely to encourage the emergence of on-rail competition along all of the more heavily trafficked lines of route. Indeed, it could be described as a 'cream skimmer's charter'. As I said earlier, open-access operators can use Railtrack's facilities as long as they can find some spare slots and are willing to pay short-run variable costs, which are typically far less than the per train costs of the franchisees.

The problems which these arrangements pose for the Regulator in deciding how much exclusivity or protection from competition to accept in access agreements have been discussed in the Consultative Document on on-rail competition issued by ORR in July 1994.[1] The Consultative Document recognised that some development of access pricing mechanisms was desirable in order to minimise the need for the Regulator to impose administered solutions which would depend heavily on the particular

---

[1]   Office of the Rail Regulator, *Competition for Railway Passenger Services: A Consultative Document*, ORR, July 1994.

circumstances of each case. However, none of the pricing options reviewed in the paper appeared to offer a clear way forward.

Long-run Marginal Cost Pricing of Infrastructure?

An option that would, I believe, substantially improve matters and which was not examined in the Consultation Document, would be to apply the well-established principles of long-run marginal or incremental cost pricing to infrastructure provision for all types of operator. Applied to the more lightly-used parts of the system, where the need for long-term replacement of the infrastructure assets was uncertain, this approach would set track usage charges equal to short-term variable costs as at present.

In the more heavily-used parts of the system, where demand is relatively intense, and where the likelihood of open-access competition emerging is strongest, all types of operator would pay both the short-run variable cost-related charges and, in addition, a charge to reflect the long-run incremental costs of providing capacity. Principles of efficient allocation of joint costs would suggest that this capacity-related charge should be levied wholly or largely on peak traffic.

Such an approach accords, as I have said, with well-established principles of utility pricing. Compared with the existing arrangements, it would have the advantages, *first*, of restricting the scope for cream-skimming competition, thus protecting the Franchising Director's budget. It would, however, achieve this in an efficient manner by removing the possibilities of inefficient competition based on underpriced access to infrastructure. *Second*, it would be clearly non-discriminatory as between different types of operator. *Third*, by increasing the variability of franchisees' costs with output it would reduce the risks faced by franchisees, possibly increasing the attractiveness of franchises and encouraging competition for them.

Weakness of the Franchising Element

Now while such a change should, I believe, improve the performance of the restructured industry, I remain sceptical about whether it would be sufficient to rescue the franchising element of the privatisation process. The difficulties currently being experienced on that front reflect the limited rôle accorded to the franchisee in the current approach.

Particularly unattractive features, I think, include the following. *First*, the extent to which the franchisee's performance depends on a single external agency in the form of Railtrack. *Second*, the limited opportunities for rent creation inherent in what amounts to a labour only contracting rôle for a very small proportion of value added. *Third*, the perceived difficulties John Swift has eloquently described in the current competitive environment.

Even under a modified track access régime of the kind that I have suggested, on-rail competition would be an uneasy affair. A set of services covered by franchise contracts would co-exist with open-access services subject to far fewer constraints or inhibitions. If the franchising process continues to founder because of these difficulties, I would expect underlying railway economics to reassert themselves and for the system to develop in either a Swedish or an Argentinian direction. Interestingly, neither model appears positively to demand the presence of a railway regulator.

The Swedish model has strong affinities with the arrangements in the stage carriage bus industry created in Great Britain following the 1985 Transport Act. By analogy, on-rail competition, or the threat of it, would restrain the conduct of train operators and competition problems could be dealt with through the Competition or Fair Trading Acts. Under the Argentinian approach, franchisees' conduct in markets where demand was relatively captive could be regulated through franchise contracts which would specify maximum fares and minimum levels of service.

In conclusion, then, I believe that John Swift can look forward to an interesting and eventful next few years, whilst the industry sorts itself out, or is sorted out. Even without politically driven changes, however, I think it is interesting to speculate whether 10 years or so hence the Beesley Lectures, as I am sure these splendid occasions will come to be called, will actually need a slot for a railway regulator.

6

THE CHARTER AIRLINE INDUSTRY: A CASE HISTORY OF SUCCESSFUL DEREGULATION

The Rt. Hon. Christopher Chataway
Civil Aviation Authority

BRITAIN'S CHARTER AIRLINE INDUSTRY is remarkable both for its size and for its competitiveness. In 1993 it carried over 25 million passengers to and from the UK – about half of UK air travel within Europe. While the airline business is and always has been characterised by a high degree of regulation, the British charter industry is probably the nearest thing yet seen in air travel to a free market. It was not always thus. In this paper I want to trace the deregulation of charter services in Britain, draw some international parallels, look at the way this healthy market has been sustained, consider the potential threats to it, and see what lessons, if any, emerge from this story for other regulators.

To someone from outside the industry it must seem extraordinary that governments maintained, and in some cases still maintain, tight controls on route entry, capacity and price for scheduled services while in many parts of the developed world charters have had a much freer rein. The original reason for this difference is probably that the founding fathers of the Chicago convention, which defined the then five freedoms of the air and set the pattern for mercantilist exchange of traffic rights, did not see charters as a significant issue.

As a result, charters were treated pragmatically. Each country decided its policy on the basis of where it saw its interest lying. Some saw the overriding objective as the protection of scheduled services or of their flag carrier (in practice often the same thing), and banned them altogether. Others saw the value of cheap mass travel for inwards tourism or did not feel able to deny their own citizens the opportunity to visit and receive their friends and relatives at prices they could afford.

Boundaries Between Scheduled Services and Charters

The question of where, if at all, boundaries should be drawn between scheduled services and charters was already a major issue 25 years ago when the Edwards Committee made its recommendations for the future of British civil aviation in 1969.[1] The Committee noted that the share of non-scheduled operations in world air traffic had doubled from 8 per cent of passenger miles in 1960 to 15 per cent in 1967, by when the figure for Europe was almost a quarter. Edwards quoted Spain as a particularly striking example. Charters had carried 36 per cent of passengers to Spain in 1962, but their share had risen to 58 per cent by 1967.

Inclusive Tour Charters

As early as the 1960s the CAA's predecessor, the Air Transport Licensing Board (ATLB), was licensing inclusive tour charters (ITs) freely. However, the scope of charters was limited by what were called 'rules of charterworthiness'. Most charters were either inclusive tours or affinity group charters (AGs). The ATLB insisted that the operators of ITs charged for their total package (transport and accommodation) a sum no less than the lowest applicable fare for a scheduled service on the route concerned. This, known as 'Provision 1', was already under attack by the time Edwards reported. Edwards noted that Provision 1 was already under strain because of the introduction of tours to more distant destinations where fares were very high, and because of attempts to develop low-price winter tours. There was a particular problem when IATA heavily increased fares from the UK as a result of devaluation in 1967, but the tour operators saw no need for a corresponding increase in IT prices. In 1968, the President of the Board of Trade relaxed the system by allowing certain tours for only 50 or 60 per cent of the lowest scheduled fare.

The ATLB was keen to maintain minimum prices and said it wished to preserve holiday standards, to prevent the collapse of too many tour companies or airlines, to maintain operating standards and safety, and to prevent erosion of traffic from scheduled services. Edwards, however, thought that this view was too restrictionist and recommended that, whilst scheduled services should be protected, this should be only where there was a public policy case for doing so.

Affinity Group Charters

The other main form of charter, both to Europe and elsewhere, was the affinity group. The idea was that members of clubs whose purpose was not air travel could charter aircraft. Many clubs took advantage of this,

---

1 *British Air Transport in the Seventies* (Chairman: Professor Sir Ronald Edwards, KBE), Cmnd.4018, London: HMSO, 1969.

one of the more often quoted examples being the Trowbridge and District Caged Birds Society. By the time the CAA was established in 1971 the charterworthiness rules were falling into further disrepute. The affinity groups became a joke. There were sporadic attempts to police them, but they were sold through a range of agencies. Technically there was a six-months membership qualification period but some passengers joined the groups on the airport bus and others not at all. Similarly, even the relaxed Provision 1 became ineffective as tour operators, being unable to discount the price legally, added value in the form of free car hire, free drinks, free duty free, and so on. The CAA abolished Provision 1 in 1973.

But that was not all. Once price was no longer regulated a new loophole was created since the rules required accommodation to be sold with the package but did not define what accommodation was. In 1976 the CAA decided against intervening to restrict low-cost inclusive tours. Soon people were being offered accommodation in dormitories and even in caves. Some tour operators went out of their way to explain how substandard the accommodation was, and the next step was to levy service charges on those who did choose to use it.

As a result the UK scheduled airlines, principally British Airways (BA), pointed out with some justice that the CAA's inability or unwillingness to enforce charterworthiness rules meant that they were no longer being given the protection hitherto thought at least partly necessary if they were to maintain scheduled services. BA pulled out of a number of Mediterranean routes, including important holiday destinations such as Corfu and Palma, but continued to fly to most of them on a charter basis through a lower-cost subsidiary, British Airtours, and by using mainline aircraft at weekends. By this time the scheduled airlines were already matching charter prices, or coming close to matching them, through part-charter fares – in effect by selling blocks of seats to tour organisers in more or less the same way as whole plane charters were sold.

'Group 3' Fares

In 1975 BA invented another competitive response – the 'Group 3' fare. At that time it was taking delivery of Tristar aircraft against what turned out to be a weak market, and it therefore sought to meet charter competition while not diluting its higher-fare traffic. It came up with the device of a cheap fare available without buying a package, but only for people travelling in groups of at least three. This was the signal for the charter airlines to seek regulatory protection. They argued that BA was cross-subsidising from other sources and dumping excess capacity into the market at the expense of lower-cost charter specialists. After a bitterly contested public hearing, the CAA decided that Group 3 was a legitimate competitive response but reiterated that the basic concept of the scheduled service should be preserved by insisting that no more than half the capacity of a scheduled aircraft should be sold on a charter basis. As things turned out the Group 3 idea, although clever, was not a success and was soon dropped.

In 1982 the CAA announced a new concept by which charter airlines could offer up to 15 per cent of their seats on a quasi-scheduled basis, without accommodation, on certain routes. This modest proposal, designed to give people the benefit of more flexible arrangements on routes served mainly by charters, received a dusty response from most of Europe.

Following a major review of airline policy ahead of the privatisation of BA, the 1984 Airline Competition White Paper[2] emphasised the need to continue to allow BA to serve all markets but to preserve safeguards against anti-competitive behaviour. In 1985 Britannia and several other airlines sought to limit the capacity BA could offer in the charter market. The CAA did not accept Britannia's proposal because, while there was little doubt about BA's ability to dominate the charter market should it choose to do so, there was insufficient evidence of actual, as opposed to potential, damage to charters and it was clear that users benefited from the range of products BA offered.

Liberalisation of the Air, 1993

When the third package took effect in January 1993, the scheduled/charter distinction in Europe became academic for regulatory purposes since airlines were now free to offer the products and prices they wished. Airlines and tour operators are no longer bound by charterworthiness rules. Their passengers can go out on one airline and come back on another, travel out to one destination and back from another, buy ground arrangements or not buy ground arrangements, and so on. As yet the holiday industry has been slow to widen its range of products to take advantage of these new freedoms, but there is nothing to stop it from doing so where profitable opportunities exist.

Charters on Long-Haul Routes

The story on long-haul routes is different in some important respects. Here charters grew up not primarily to fly passengers on inclusive tours but to provide cheap travel for independent travellers, including many students and people visiting friends and relatives.

---

2 Department of Transport, *Airline Competition Policy*, Cmnd. 9366, London: HMSO, October 1984.

Initially, most long-haul charters were the infamous affinity group charters. They served a public demand but because of the Byzantine arrangements under which most passengers were technically travelling illegally, they were insufficient to meet the full market demand and questionable in their integrity. Their shadiness sometimes attracted less than fastidious operators. The solution eventually came through the Advance Booking Charter (ABC). The scheduled airlines, particularly BA, had already developed the concept of the APEX fare by which they could both differentiate between high-yield and low-yield passengers and, by careful management of price and capacity, offer leisure passengers lower but still cost-related fares. At the CAA, Ray Colegate saw this principle as a way of both clearing away the murky world of North Atlantic affinities while enabling charters to offer a more attractive product. Although there were later adaptations, the main rule governing ABCs was the requirement to book in advance.

Charters never developed as the main form of low-cost travel across the Atlantic. This is mainly because the cost advantages which charters generally have over scheduled services on short-haul routes are not so pronounced on long-haul routes. The direct costs of flying the aircraft are a much higher proportion of total cost on long-haul routes. As a result, some of the costs which are much lower on charters or which charters avoid altogether – especially in the sales, reservations and passenger handling area – are less significant on long haul. Furthermore, seating densities are more or less the same in the back cabins of scheduled aircraft as on charters and both work at similar rates of seat occupancy. Thus the sustainable fares for charters and scheduled passengers on leisure services tend to be similar, which means that an airline aiming at the low-fare market does not necessarily have to operate in charter mode.

The most obvious example of this was Sir Freddy Laker's Skytrain. Before Skytrain, charters were more important, peaking at around 25 per cent of UK/US traffic, but this reflected the more stringent bilateral restrictions of the time and the initial reluctance of both the UK and the US Governments to allow low fares on scheduled routes. Once Sir Freddy got his designation from the UK Government and his permit from the US Government he was able, in effect, to use his former charter traffic as the platform for Skytrain. Thus charters now have only a very small share of the North Atlantic market and are concentrated mainly on package holiday destinations, especially Florida.

Charter Standards and Threat to Scheduled Services

As I mentioned at the beginning, the main concerns of those who were cautious about further liberalisation of charters were that scheduled services would be reduced or driven off altogether and that standards of service (and in this context some people included safety standards) would be undermined.

On the first point, it is quite true that the traditional scheduled airlines, including BA at that time, were not able to continue service on all routes in the face of increasingly strong charter competition. It is now many years since it has flown scheduled services to Heraklion, Corfu, Palma or the Canary Islands, although it is interesting to note that British Midland (BM) now does fly to Palma. But I doubt whether protection from charters would have allowed BA to maintain those services for much longer. Given the very small proportion of passengers on these routes who would be prepared to pay the full scheduled fare to maintain an on-demand service, to restrict charters in their interests alone would be to let the tail wag the dog. In this context, it is relevant that a few years ago BA withdrew from Ireland, not because of charter competition but because of the low yields. However, BA and other scheduled airlines do operate to those leisure destinations such as Malaga and Faro where there are far more people who want the traditional scheduled product and are prepared to pay for it, and they continue to offer part-charter on these flights.

On long-haul routes, I think recent history shows that efficient scheduled airlines tend to have the upper hand when they do battle with efficient charter airlines. The presence of charters on the North Atlantic stirred up the scheduled carriers and made them far more responsive to the needs of low-fare passengers. Charters will still operate, especially on purely leisure routes, and will continue to exercise a powerful discipline against scheduled airlines lowering standards or raising fares. Nevertheless, it is unlikely that they will recover their pre-Skytrain market share.

Quality and Safety

On quality, the presence of so many low-yield passengers has led airlines to be particularly attentive to persuading their high-fare passengers that they are getting value for money, and as far as service in the back cabin of short-haul aircraft is concerned, the UK charter airlines generally offer standards which, seat pitch apart, are at least the equal of many of their scheduled counterparts.

I think the safety argument is, and always was, misdirected. If the suggestion is that low-fare charter airlines will be less profitable and thus less safe, this proposition falls at the first fence because it is generally the charter airlines which have been more profitable and which, incidentally, have been able to introduce modern aircraft more rapidly than many foreign scheduled airlines. More fundamentally, we insist on the highest safety standards in the UK and I see no difference in best practice between good scheduled airlines and good charter airlines.

Benefits to Users: Comparisons with USA

How can we measure the benefits to the user? We know that around 15 million return trips were made in 1993 on international charters to or from the UK, plus an unknown number on charter-competitive fares on scheduled services. We do not know, and cannot know, how many such journeys would have been made and at what price and quality if things had been different.

The most natural comparison is with the deregulated domestic market in the USA. The USA offers some interesting parallels but also major differences. Dealing with the differences first, the US effectively banned inclusive tour charters and what it called one-stop charters before deregulation in 1978; also it prohibited integration between airlines and tour operators. Thus, although there were military charters, there never really was a domestic charter industry. Low-cost airlines, notably Southwest in Texas and PSA in California, had developed within states on routes which were not subject to CAB control and their efficiency and low fares were one of the main catalysts for inter-state deregulation.

Following deregulation in 1978, airlines not only had no charter tradition, but also there was no need to operate in the charter mode. The low-cost airlines developed by offering simpler and cheaper products, using many of the cost savings which were already associated in Europe with charters. One of the main savings came through not offering conventionally high standards of seat availability, and thus achieving seat occupancy upwards of 80 per cent rather than the 60 per cent or so associated with most scheduled services. Other examples are high seating densities, simple point-to-point fare structures without proration, and the omission of some services such as interlining, meals, baggage transfer and – in the case of People Express – baggage handling.

A recent study of Southwest, the most successful of the US low-cost airlines, showed that the average fare paid was only a little over half of that on the major airlines on flights of comparable distance. The same study also looked at costs and, after doing what it could to eliminate distortions caused by Southwest's much lower average stage length, found that its rivals, apart from America West, had costs which were higher by 50-70 per cent.

Such comparisons are broadly recognisable in the UK. If costs specific to scheduled services – that is, sales, advertising and commission – are excluded from BA's total expenses and revenue from cargo carriage is treated as a cost offset, a very rough calculation suggests that BA's costs are some two-thirds higher than those of a typical charter operator. Although the orders of magnitude are similar it would be wrong to draw the conclusion that the differences between the inherent costs of the conventional and low-cost modes are also similar. The differences between the products offered by a UK charter operator and BA operating as a scheduled operator are greater than those between Southwest and its US rivals even when distribution costs are eliminated. However, we can conclude that the liberalisation of charters in the UK and deregulation in the USA has enabled airlines to offer different, usually lower cost, types of service. This has not only widened choice but has put competitive pressure on the pre-existing more conventional airlines. In the USA the major airlines are seeking to capture Southwest's successful formula. Part of their answer is to set up low-cost subsidiaries. Similarly, I have little doubt that the need to maintain its presence in the leisure as well as the business markets under increasingly liberal charter rules has been one of the factors in BA's development from its unpromising position in the 1970s to its world leadership in the 1990s.

Liberalisation and Market Pressure

I suspect that if we had been more cautious and more inclined to give weight to what airlines, both scheduled and charter, were saying to us than we did to user interests, the sheer pressure of the market would still have forced liberalisation in the end. As noted at the beginning of this paper, such pressures were already strong even in the days of the ATLB and the early days of the CAA. However, a slower pace of change would have meant that more people would have had to wait longer for the benefits of competition and choice. On the other hand, I also believe that the gradual but still forward approach was not only necessary in terms of gaining international acceptance for liberalisation but also enabled the industry to evolve in a way which made it possible for both scheduled and charter airlines to adjust to changing circumstances. More importantly, it also enabled them to cross the boundaries of each other's products and compete effectively while having to respect the dividing line between competitive and anti-competitive behaviour.

Here again there is a parallel with the US domestic market. Although there was a short-lived attempt to liberalise in stages, in the event there was a big bang. The first few years were dramatic, with the market being widened by some high-profile new entrants, or erstwhile local airlines expanding beyond state boundaries. There were several mergers, consolidations and also bankruptcies. The larger airlines saw their competitive strength in the development of hub-and-spoke services, in some cases making major changes to their networks.

In the event most of the new entrants, the main and most conspicuous exception being Southwest, did not survive, and, although more competitive than before in some respects, the industry became more and not less concentrated in terms of the market shares of the largest airlines. Part of the reason for this is that incumbent airlines took vigorous and often closely targeted action to undermine the new entrants. Whether or not this action amounted to anti-competitive behaviour was never tested. At that time the US authorities believed that predatory behaviour was not logically possible, and that, even if it were, the market was contestable and there was no point in driving out one new entrant because, to the extent that a commercial opportunity existed, it would soon be succeeded by another.

To put it kindly, I believe that almost everyone now would recognise that view of how markets behave as very optimistic. It does seem that deregulation has served the US air traveller well, but I suspect that competition and choice might have been wider still if a closer eye had been kept on the means by which large airlines can set out to eliminate competition from smaller ones.

Charter Services – Success and Failure

The more measured pace of liberalisation of charters in the UK did not mean that airlines and tour operators were shielded from the consequences of their own decisions. Moving to open markets, whether in charter air services, scheduled air services or in industry generally, must almost by definition mean that the industry is more fluid, with some companies prospering and others failing. Indeed there is a long list of airlines, both scheduled and charter, which have benefited the user while they operated, and in some cases have left a lasting mark, but which have failed. The obvious ones are Laker, Air Europe, BCal and Dan-Air. This is also true of the tour operating industry.

Free markets bring diversity and choice, but they also mean that companies may suddenly go out of business. In an industry where people pay sometimes substantial sums 'up front' before their holiday, the Government had long recognised the case for protecting users against failures of tour operators and airlines. The consumer protection afforded by the ATOL system and the Air Travel Trust was an important, and arguably an essential, concomitant of liberalisation. In any industry in which customers pay large sums in advance for a product which some companies will inevitably not survive long enough to deliver and which has been liberalised to inject the vitality which only the market can bring, this is a general principle which must apply.

Regulator's Rôle: Long-term User Benefits from Liberalisation

Turning now to the part played by the regulator in all this, two significant conclusions emerge. *First*, the regulator had to force the pace faster than the industry would like, but not so fast as to prejudice the chance of international acceptance. We have to remember that until recently several EC countries were threatening to repatriate charter passengers who arrived without prebooked and 'proper' accommodation. As recently as 1992, airlines were still being fined for breaches of the charter rules. Indeed, such things still happen in some non-EC countries.

Industry pressure was strong and plausible on both sides. On the one hand, the scheduled airlines argued that the quality of their services to leisure destinations would fall and that some would be withdrawn altogether. On the other hand, the charter airlines, partly out of legitimate fear for what BA and others *might* do to them, sought to erect barriers against the scheduled airlines' participation in the charter market which would have muted competition between the two modes and thus denied people the benefit of choice. I firmly believe that keeping a proper distance from industry pressures and concentrating on long-term user needs is less difficult for a regulator, who is mercifully at least one stage removed from the political process, than it would be for a government department.

The *second* main conclusion is that the benefits of liberalisation flow not just from the sector being liberalised but from the competitive interplay between it and its more regulated counterpart. Just as the CAA resisted the scheduled airlines' argument that they should be less exposed to competition, so too did it resist the pressures from the charter airlines to erect new fences to protect them. The aim always was to create a climate in which the two modes could compete directly, with the best and most suitable succeeding in individual markets. In this I think we were successful.

That is not to say that all our problems are necessarily behind us. Recent experience has shown that large, powerful airlines have important advantages and that their influence is increasing. As we said in the decision on Britannia's application to limit BA's charter activity in 1986, large, strong airlines have the potential to weaken, and even to drive out, smaller ones. That said, I see no more evidence now than there was then that this is actually happening. We have several large and strong charter airlines, some of which are themselves backed by powerful groups, and several new charter airlines have emerged and are operating successfully. Several big flag carriers have quite deliberately decided to concentrate on developing and maintaining scheduled networks rather than become involved in very low-cost services to which they are not suited.

Another recent development has been increasing vertical integration within the travel business between its three main tiers, the retail agents, tour operators and charter airlines. In the UK one tour operator, Thomson, leads the market with 24 per cent of the passengers carried, followed by Owners Abroad and Airtours with around 13 per cent each and Cosmos with 8 per cent. These four companies also own charter airlines. However, there are many others, including other major players in each tier of the market. New operators are still entering both the tour market and the charter airline industry. In these days of the Single Market we might also expect more competition across national boundaries than there is now.

Conclusions

I remain optimistic about the future strength and competitiveness of the charter industry, but we are not, I hope, complacent. I have identified several ways in which the underlying structure of the airline and leisure travel industries could lead to concentration and to dominant operators seeking to bring unacceptable pressure to bear on their smaller rivals. We must maintain the powers which exist both in London and in Brussels to deal with monopolistic or predatory behaviour and, while remaining properly reluctant to interfere in what by aviation standards, and perhaps by any standard, is a successful free market, we should not be afraid to use them.

This paper has been about a particular part of a particular industry. But I chose this subject because I felt it might find echoes in most sectors of the economy which have been or are being liberalised. The watchword for the regulator is to maintain his independence and to take on board the pleadings of producers only insofar as they are congruent with the needs of users. Most of these industries have dominant, and often increasingly efficient, traditional players and this adds emphasis to the regulator's task of ensuring that smaller enterprises and new entrants are neither unfairly forced out of the market nor insulated from the market's disciplines.

DISCUSSANT'S COMMENTS

Professor Rigas Doganis
Cranfield University

THIS PAPER IS STIMULATING AND IMPORTANT in two respects: *first*, because the charter industry is an aviation sector which is rarely commented on or discussed; *second*, because of its early deregulation, as Christopher Chataway pointed out, it is an industry which perhaps has lessons both for the scheduled airline industry and for other sectors as well.

It is sometimes forgotten that the British charter airlines are significantly larger in many cases than other well-known scheduled airlines. To give you an example, Britannia, in terms of international traffic, is more significant and larger than SAS. It is two-and-a-half times the size of Sabena. It is, in terms of world ranking, the 17th largest international airline, and yet it is a charter airline. Very often we think of the charter airlines as being second best or somehow being a secondary sector of aviation. Not so – it is a major sector of aviation. Within the European market, something like two-thirds of international air traffic in Europe travels on charter flights, not on scheduled flights. As the paper pointed out, it is the sector of the air transport industry which has been progressively liberalised since the mid- to late-1960s.

The 'Third Package' – Fundamental Differences

Against that background many points arise from the paper because it was clearly far-reaching and wide-ranging. I would like just to pick two or three for further discussion. One of the claims made in the paper is that the scheduled/charter distinction in Europe has become largely academic for regulatory purposes since the introduction of the 'third package'. The 'third package' of liberalisation measures in Europe came into force in January 1993. One key element of that package was to see no distinction between scheduled and charter. Therefore, all the regulations, or lack of them, affecting scheduled apply equally to charter.

To what extent is this true? I think there are two respects in which it is not quite true. *First*, the charter and the scheduled industry are fundamentally different in their methods of distribution. By that I mean that the charter airlines sell primarily to tour operators and travel agents. They sell some seats on a seat-only basis, without a package holiday involved, but even that is usually sold directly by the charterer – that is, the person, the tour operator, or the travel agent which initially chartered the aircraft.

Conversely, the scheduled airlines market is quite different. They sell primarily in the open markets and to individuals. They also sell through travel agents. The implications of that, I think, are quite important and may have implications as far as regulation is concerned. They are that charter airlines usually sell their capacity a year in advance. In other words, the charter airlines have already sold their capacity for the summer of 1995. In fact, they sold it in June and July of 1994. Having sold that capacity, they can then set about providing it. In many cases they will have sold seats in aircraft that they do not actually yet own or operate. So they are in a situation which is very easy for them.

Compare that to the situation of the scheduled airline that has to put the capacity into the market and then sell it. In other words, they have to start flying and then try to sell the seats once they are committed to a schedule of services. Now that may mean that the two sectors will not fuse; there will continue to be differences between them.

Effects of Liberalisation on Charter/Scheduled Competition

Second, despite the efforts of the Civil Aviation Authority and the European Commission, in practice the two sectors of the industry have come closer but have not actually merged in terms of their operations. As a result of liberalisation, the major charter airlines were expected to provide a major source of competition for the large scheduled airlines. They have not done so. Where they have tried to enter into scheduled markets in a significant way, as Air Europe and Dan Air did, they have collapsed.

So we find that the charter airlines are only operating in a small number of scheduled markets, usually where there is not strong scheduled competition, and invariably to holiday destinations. We do not see charter airlines flying between London and Glasgow, or London and Paris; we see one on London-Amsterdam, but it is on a very small basis, and largely flying on behalf of a scheduled carrier.

To give just one example, at one stage in the process of liberalisation Britannia had 19 route licences for scheduled operations. It operated only one and has subsequently pulled out of that. Thus, while as far as leisure markets are concerned, the charters and the scheduled services do overlap, I believe the pattern of operations is sufficiently different to ensure two distinct industrial sectors.

Can a businessman take advantage of cheap charter flights to go to Athens as he can in the United States to fly on South West? He cannot. The inconveniences of doing so are such that he has to travel on a scheduled flight. Thus, I think one may challenge the contention in the paper that the CAA was successful in its aim 'to create a climate in which the two modes could compete directly' (above, p.94). I believe the two modes do compete but they do not compete directly and they do not compete in all sectors of the market.

The paper rightly points out that the UK charter industry is characterised by both market concentration and vertical integration. The top four tour operators generate about 60 per cent of the business in passenger numbers and the top three airlines also generate about 60 per cent of the charter market. In fact, the three top airlines are themselves directly linked with tour operators.

However, in the charter market the degree of concentration has not increased significantly over the last 10 or 15 years. The airlines at the top have changed, but the level of concentration has not changed. On the other hand, directly as a result of liberalisation in Europe, we find that the degree and level of concentration within the industry as a whole is increasing very markedly.

Concentration of Airline Groups Following Liberalisation

I have taken the airline groupings as they were in 1993 and in most cases as they still are, and have worked out what percentage of the European scheduled market those airlines together controlled, either in terms of passenger kilometres or passenger numbers. When I did this, only the 1992 traffic figures were available, so the measures take the 1993 groupings, but look at their shares in terms of 1992.

First, a number of airlines have grouped together, either through shareholdings, mergers, or, in some cases, through code sharing as well. None of these airlines were together five or six years ago. So the process of agglomeration and concentration is a direct consequence of liberalisation. Within Europe, the top six groups have nearly three-quarters of the market. Five or six years earlier, the top six airlines had about 60 per cent of the market. And if the Alcathazar project had gone ahead the level of concentration would have increased to about 80 per cent. In other words, the top six airlines would have controlled 80 per cent of the traffic within Europe. And although the Alcathazar merger did not take place, I am sure within a year or two something else will come along to replace it.

That is one way of looking at concentration. Another way of looking at concentration and the impact of deregulation is to study the number of routes on which there are more than two competitors. I have taken the 20 busiest routes in Europe on scheduled services, in the expectation that it is on the busiest routes that you would expect to find the greatest competition. More than half the busiest routes in Europe are out of London. The average number of airlines on those routes had risen to four in 1989, but since then the average has slowly declined, partly because airlines have gone out of business, partly because of mergers and take-overs and franchising of smaller carriers by larger airlines.

If one takes out of the picture airlines which appear to be competitive but are not independent because they are owned by other carriers, the average number of carriers per route in 1994 was only three, and on several important routes, like London-Geneva, or London-Rome, there are effectively only two carriers. The prices of those two carriers, particularly in the business sector, are invariably the same. Even where there are three or four carriers, very often the prices are the same.

In other markets, for example in Scandinavia where there are three very busy markets, it is only in the last year that we have had two airlines competing. But again, as duopolists, they have no incentive to compete on price. There is a strong inducement to collude tacitly on tariffs. On the routes out of Paris, there are on average less than three airlines per route, and on many of them there are only two carriers.

Now the reason for this concentration is that there are significant barriers to entry within the scheduled sector. In many cases, the barriers to entry are related to the difficulties of marketing, not to the cost disadvantages of the new entrant. I would like to emphasise particularly the inadequacy of runway slots – the inability of competitors to get slots when they want to enter a market. To give just one example: British Midland wanted to compete on London-Paris with Air France and British Airways out of Heathrow; the only way it could get the slots to do that was to stop flying to Liverpool. So Liverpool, which had seven flights a day to London, lost all its services to London in order that the number of services from London to Paris should go up from 25 to 32.

What is happening in the scheduled market in Europe raises the greatest concern. Mr Chataway stated that for the US air traveller, 'competition and choice might have been wider still if a closer eye had been kept on the means by which large airlines can set out to eliminate competition from smaller ones' (above, p.93). It seems to me this is precisely what is now happening in Europe.

Are the Regulatory Powers of the CAA Really Necessary?

Finally, he argued that one must maintain the powers which exist in London and Brussels to deal with monopolistic and predatory behaviour. This seems to me to beg two questions which are worthy of further discussion.

The *first* is, can one identify predatory behaviour in the airline industry, particularly in relation to pricing? The marginal cost of carrying an extra passenger on a scheduled flight that is due to depart in an hour's time for Paris is very low. It is, effectively, the airport's passenger tax, or passenger charge, and some extra fuel. Now, if the marginal cost is very low, and if at the same time the whole emphasis of deregulated markets is that we should have yield-management programmes, where the aim of the airline is not to worry about the fare from each individual passenger, but to be concerned about maximising the revenue from a flight as a whole, can one really identify predatory pricing in the airline industry? If one cannot, then a regulator to monitor it may not be necessary.

The *second* question arising out of the statement in the paper is: What should be the balance of regulatory powers between the civil aviation authorities in London and Brussels? Does the CAA have any rôle at all as a regulator when the key decisions are increasingly made by the European Commission and the European Court of Justice?

Perhaps the rôle of the CAA is merely to implement and monitor regulations and decisions taken elsewhere – by the Commission as far as economic regulations are concerned, by the joint airworthiness authorities as far as technical and safety regulation is concerned. In other words, is the Civil Aviation Authority in its twilight years? Is it soon going to disappear below the horizon?

7

COMPETITION IN ELECTRICITY: RETROSPECT AND PROSPECT

Professor Stephen Littlechild
Office of Electricity Regulation

Introduction

THE INTRODUCTION OF COMPETITION has been the distinctive feature of the privatisation of electricity. The title of this lecture invites me to consider how far this has been achieved and what more needs to be done. It is not possible in one short paper to cover all the aspects of competition. For example, I shall not have space to cover the major and increasingly critical area of competition in supply, with all the implications for 1998. Nonetheless, the three areas I intend to cover should provide enough food for thought. I shall concentrate on competition in generation, the greater contribution the nuclear sector can make to this, and the appropriate rôle of transmission and distribution networks in facilitating competition.

Competition in Generation

An effective competitive market in generation has been a fundamental aim of electricity privatisation from the very beginning. For several reasons it was not able to be achieved at Vesting. Plant accounting for 78 per cent of pre-Vesting output in England and Wales was given to the two largest successor companies, and 94 per cent to the three largest. The Secretary of State and the Director General were both given a statutory duty to promote competition in generation. In contrast to telecoms and gas, this duty was given prominence. The task was actively to ensure the development of the generation sector into a fully competitive market.

Competition in generation has indeed increased over the last four years, and I have taken several steps to promote it. Nevertheless, the market is not yet fully competitive. In this first section of the paper, I want to review developments to date in England and Wales and to conjecture where these developments might lead in future.

Market Shares of Output

An obvious place to start is with market shares of output. Table 1 shows the evolving position over the last five years. Nuclear Electric has continued to increase its output, to over 23 per cent of the total. Output from new entrants is now over 7 per cent. In contrast, the shares of National Power and PowerGen are down to about 34 per cent and 25 per cent respectively. The figures thus indicate a continued reduction in the market share of the so-called duopoly, now for the first time below 60 per cent. This can be expected to fall somewhat further as the new independent and nuclear capacity comes on stream. As a result of Nuclear Electric's increased market share, there has been a less marked reduction, to about 83 per cent, in the market share of the three largest companies (the 'triopoly').

Table 1: Generator Market Shares of Pooled Output, 1989/90 - 1993/94

Generator	1989/90† %	1990/91 %	1991/92 %	1992/93 %	1993/94 %	Oct 93 - Sept 94 %
National Power	48.0	45.5	43.6	41.0	35.0	34.1
PowerGen	29.7	28.4	28.1	27.1	26.1	25.3
Nuclear Electric	16.5	17.4	18.6	21.3	23.2	23.3
Inter-connectors and Pumped Storage*	4.8††	7.7	8.4	8.7	8.4	8.8
New Entrants	0.0	0.1	0.3	1.0	6.2	7.3
Others**	1.0††	1.0	0.9	0.9	1.1	1.1
TOTAL	100.0	100.0	100.0	100.0	100.0	100.0

*   Scottish Power and Scottish Hydro-Electric (via the Scottish Interconnector), Electricité de France (via the French Interconnector), and National Grid Company's Pumped Storage Business.
** Mainly British Nuclear Fuels, Atomic Energy Authority and Pooled renewables.
†   Pre-Vesting Central Electricity Generating Board.
†† Estimated.

New Entry

Another indication of the development of competition in generation is the extent of new entry. At the time of my MMC decision on the major generators, over 3,000 MW of new Combined Cycle Gas Turbine (CCGT) capacity had been commissioned and a further 2,600 MW was under construction. Since then there have been announcements of agreements to build two further CCGT stations with a total capacity of about 1,000 MW. Achieved and potential new entry presently totals some 6,900 MW of CCGT.

It had been claimed that the price cap which I introduced early in 1994 had destroyed confidence in the market and would deter further new entry, not just for the two years of the cap, but also (in view of the fear of a further price cap) for many years to come. Evidently this is not the case. Recent decisions indicate that there are new entrants who want to compete and, even after the announcement of the price cap, are prepared to commit substantial funds to do so in the expectation that future generation prices will reward relatively efficient new plant.

The decisions to build new plants may also indicate that certain market factors have moved in a direction favourable to new entry – for example, that gas supplies may now be obtained at lower prices and on more flexible terms than before. These terms may be conducive to running the plant either base load or mid-merit, depending on conditions in the electricity market. It may also be that the owners see better prospects for switching gas between the gas and electricity markets, thereby increasing their flexibility and reducing prospective risks.

Concerns about New Entry

Some have expressed concern about this further new entry, particularly those with an interest in existing plant. In particular, there have been concerns about Regional Electricity Companies (RECs) basing their investment and purchasing decisions on their captive supply markets. Let me comment briefly on these.

First, it is not as if RECs are alone in building new CCGT capacity. The established generators are doing so too. In fact, National Power and PowerGen have commissioned or have under construction over 6,300 MW of CCGT capacity, about the same as the total amount that the RECs have been involved in.

The *second* point to note is that these two latest CCGT projects have not been developed and financed in the same way as the previous independent power projects. They are not backed wholly or mainly by 15-year power purchase contracts with RECs matched by similar shares of REC ownership. Although one project is financed 25 per cent by MEB, the remainder of the output has been purchased by two independent parties: IVO from Finland and Tomen Corporation from Japan. The latter parties are investing and buying contracts for differences (CfDs)[1] on a 'merchant basis', taking the full risks of selling at whatever prices subsequently obtain in the Pool and the contracts market. As regards the other project, Eastern has indicated that it is not committing its supply business to long-term purchases of CfDs but instead envisages that its generation business will sell CfDs into the competitive market. The full details are not yet clear, but these projects seem to represent a further development of a more competitive market in generation.

The involvement in generation of public electricity suppliers who have licence monopolies in distribution and, for the present, in supply is a long-standing concern. It always has been and is likely to remain so as long as present arrangements continue. Nevertheless, the RECs' licensed monopoly of the supply market is limited to the under-100 kW market – about half the total market – and expires in 1998. Bearing in mind that it takes a couple of years to commission a new station, a decision to build a new plant now means that when the plant comes on stream there will be only one year of licence monopoly left. My aim is to ensure that, after 1998, effective competition in supply removes any residual market power of the local RECs as fast as possible.

Whilst such competition is developing, the price that RECs can charge their captive franchise customers will be constrained by their economic purchasing obligation. I shall continue to scrutinise the generation costs that RECs propose to pass through to their franchise customers, and I shall be compiling and publishing some yardstick measures of these.

My 'Further Statement on Economic Purchasing' in February 1993 concluded that assessing RECs' purchasing decisions at periodic intervals remained the best way of ensuring compliance with their licence conditions, but that it might be appropriate for me to hold more frequent economic purchasing reviews than would be associated with reviews of price controls. I still have this under consideration, together with the question whether putting out purchases to tender would be helpful.

These and other considerations would also be relevant in considering any requests to modify the REC own-generation limits. I have told the RECs that at present I do not see a sufficient case for a material change to the Vesting arrangements. However, alternative formulations of the limits might also be considered – for example, to prohibit or limit REC purchases

---

[1] Suppliers and generators wishing to hedge the financial risks associated with Pool prices are able to do so by signing bilateral contracts for differences (CfDs). CfDs are financial instruments. They do not have to be directly related to Pool prices but typically a CfD will provide for payment to the generator (seller) where Pool prices fall below a predetermined level and payment to the supplier (purchaser) where Pool prices exceed a predetermined level. The precise form of the CfD is a matter for the parties involved.

from a generation company in which it has an equity interest. A further possibility is mentioned at the end of this paper.[2]

Market Shares of Capacity

Against the signs of increasing competition in generation, we have to note certain qualifications. For example, Table 2 shows that market shares in terms of capacity are changing at a slower rate than shares in terms of output.

Table 2: Generator Market Shares of Capacity, 1994

Generator	Shares of		
	Capacity at Vesting %	Present Capacity* %	Future Capacity** %
National Power	48	39	37
PowerGen	30	30	28
Nuclear Electric	14	16	15
Inter-connectors and Pumped Storage	8	9	8
New entrants	0	5	10
Others	0	1	1
Total	100	100	100

* Present capacity includes temporary closures.

** 'Future' capacity is defined as present capacity including closures plus capacity under construction less capacity notified for permanent closure. This is an indicative figure only, and actual capacity will depend on many considerations.

It is true that National Power and PowerGen have closed significant amounts of capacity. The extent of this has increased since my MMC decision in February 1994. As of November 1994, the two companies have closed some 14,500 MW of capacity and notified a further 2,000 MW for

---

2 *Editor's Note:* In January 1995 the Director General conducted that it would be reasonable to consider a REC's request to increase its own-generation limit on condition that it accepted explicit restrictions on the contracts it signed with its supply business, and at a minimum would be prohibited from passing additional own-generation contracts into its franchise market. (Offer Press Release R2/95).

closure. They have indicated that they may decide to close more. But a quarter of the closed plant is only temporarily mothballed, and at the same time, as noted above, National Power and PowerGen have built or have under construction about as much new capacity as all the other new entrants put together.

At Vesting, National Power and PowerGen had about 78 per cent of the capacity in the industry, the same as their attributed share of output. They presently have about 69 per cent of the total capacity, and on the basis of capacity under construction and notified for permanent closure their capacity share will still be about 65 per cent. In round terms, their share of total capacity is falling only half as fast as their share of total output.

Greater availability of capacity, including by bringing up to 3,600 MW of plant out of mothballs, gives these two companies greater flexibility in the market. They have a potential for expanding output, either in the event of an upturn in demand or otherwise, which other companies do not have. This gives them greater influence on the size of the capacity margin and the associated capacity payments in the Pool.

In short, the development of competition in generation is not reflected only in the market shares of output. Shares of capacity are also important in assessing competition. These suggest a yet greater degree of market power on the part of the two major generators than market shares of output do.

Baseload and Non-Baseload Output

The new entry that has taken place and is in prospect for the future has until recently been almost entirely geared to running baseload. This is fine as far as it goes, but it does mean that competition to run in the non-baseload section of the load curve is still limited almost entirely to the two major generators. To illustrate this, Figure 1 shows a time-of-day load curve for the year as a whole, showing the patterns of output of the different generators. The outputs of Nuclear Electric, the independent CCGTs and the interconnectors are practically constant throughout the day. It is the plant owned by National Power and PowerGen that accounts for almost all the variation in output by time of day.

To express this numerically, I have calculated the market shares of baseload output, defined as average output in the 8-hour night-time period (11:00 p.m. to 7:00 a.m.), and assumed this to be continued throughout the day-time period also. I have then calculated market shares for the remaining output (non-baseload) during the day-time period (7:00 a.m. to 11:00 p.m.). On this basis, baseload output is about 86 per cent of total output. Although non-baseload output accounts for only about 14 per cent of the total output, it is a crucial component which, *inter alia*, sets Pool price during the highest-

Fig. 1: Market Shares by Time of Day: Total Output, 1993/94

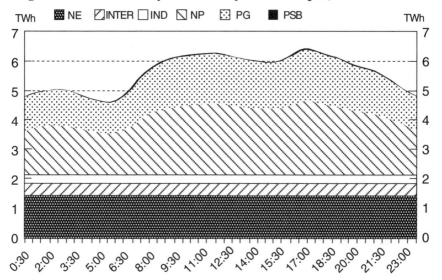

price two-thirds of the day, and enables contributing generators to offer contracts for differences better tailored to the load curve over that critical period.

The calculations show that National Power and PowerGen supplied about 55 per cent of baseload output in 1993/94, slightly less than their share of total output. But their share of non-baseload output was no less than 95 per cent. The increased output by Nuclear Electric and the interconnectors, and the new entry by independents, has changed market shares of baseload output, but has so far had little or no impact on market shares for the non-baseload part of the load curve.

It is true that plant forced out of baseload running may put increased competitive pressure on plant running mid-merit, and displaced mid-merit plant may in turn put increased pressure on plant running at peak. But all the plant involved is owned by National Power and Powergen. The extent and distribution of capacity is subject to their own decisions on closure and mothballing.

The two companies are thus competing only with each other for a critical part of the load curve. It is possible that National Power's share of non-baseload output may have declined slightly over time relative to PowerGen's. But no entry has yet taken place, or is immediately in prospect, to change their dominance there.

Sale or Disposal of Plant

These various considerations emphasise the need to introduce more competition in the generation market, particularly in certain parts of it, more quickly than would otherwise occur. Hence my proposal to the two major generators in February 1994 that they should undertake to sell or dispose of 6,000 MW of coal-fired or oil-fired plant by December 1995. Both companies accepted these undertakings.

I have since received reports from the two companies and have discussed these with them at some length. I understand that discussions are still taking place between each of the two companies and certain potential purchasers. It would not be appropriate at this stage to comment further on the state of play. I would emphasise, however, that I continue to attach the greatest importance to promoting a fully competitive market in generation as the best way of protecting customers. The sale or disposal of coal or oil-fired plant by the two major generators was explicitly designed to introduce more independent competitors, able to challenge the ability of the two major generators to increase prices, with the aim of bringing about an industry that would not be vulnerable to the exercise of market power. So the sale or disposal of plant is an integral part of achieving a more competitive generating industry. If the sales or disposals are not completed, or do not look likely to be completed within the specified time, then I shall have to consider again the possibility of a reference to the MMC.

Nuclear Electricity

In my submission to the Government's Nuclear Review, I examined the nuclear sector of the British electricity industry and made several recommendations for policy. I will now briefly review the main conclusions as they apply to competition in England and Wales.

Nuclear Electric's market share of output has increased from below 17 per cent before Vesting to over 23 per cent, and may soon overtake PowerGen's. It already supplies more baseload output than PowerGen. As Sizewell B comes on stream, and its reactor performance continues to improve, its market share is likely to increase further. The company's Finance Director has speculated that Nuclear Electric could be the largest generator in England and Wales from next year onwards.

Nuclear Electric has argued that it is simply a price taker, and therefore has no market power. I do not accept this. It may have little direct influence on non-baseload prices, but being content to let others set the lead in setting system marginal price (SMP) does not mean it has no market power. In deciding its output policy, it has to take account of the effect of its policy on other generators and on Pool prices, and other generators in turn must take account of Nuclear Electric's strategy, so the company does influence Pool prices directly. It also has an important rôle in the contracts market, where it is able to exert a significant degree of influence more directly by virtue of its market share.

For various reasons, Nuclear Electric has not yet achieved its commitment to offer sufficient contracts for differences to ensure that its net position covers the bulk of its mean expected output. Its proportion of output contracted has been significantly below the proportions of other generators. I have previously expressed concern about the lack of effective choice in the contracts market, and suggested that Nuclear Electric's limited contribution to this market may have been a significant factor in restricting the availability of contracts and maintaining higher prices than would otherwise have obtained. This remains a concern.

The Nuclear Review sought comments on introducing private sector finance into the nuclear industry, including the possibility of privatisation. I suggested in my submission that there would be benefits in this, provided that the nuclear companies were not subsidised in such a way as to distort their output, pricing and investment decisions.

I also argued that there would be great merit in a clearer separation of those aspects of nuclear power that receive special support from those that can operate on a fully commercial level manner. Nuclear Electric has proposed that a new privatised company should own and operate its PWR and AGR stations, while the Magnox plants would be retained within the public sector but operated by the privatised company until they are decommissioned. However, Nuclear Electric's proposal has the disadvantage that the privatised part of Nuclear Electric would retain control over the output of all existing plant. This would mean no improvement in the extent of competition. A preferable option (provided it entailed no additional subsidy) would be to ensure that all the commercial decisions for Magnox plant were the responsibility of the separate Magnox company. This would be equivalent to a market share in England and Wales of around 8 per cent, and would thereby enhance competition over the remaining lives of the Magnox plant.

A further desirable development would be to reconsider the ownership of the AGR and PWR nuclear plants in Britain with a view to promoting competition and protecting customers against the nuclear companies' market power. One option would be to transfer some of Nuclear Electric's AGR plants to Scottish Nuclear. For example, the transfer of two AGRs to Scottish Nuclear would establish the latter company as a new competitor in England and Wales, with a market share of around 6 per cent. Competition in Scotland could also be enhanced by the further transfer of one of Scottish Nuclear's plants to Nuclear Electric.

The details of such options require further thought, and I recognise that the Government will have many and wider considerations to take into account. Nevertheless, a restructuring of the two nuclear companies would minimise the difficulties associated with the present subsidy, further enhance competition in generation, reduce regulatory concerns and promote greater efficiency, all to the benefit of customers. Such restructuring would be useful, and perhaps necessary, whatever the ownership of the nuclear sector. The Nuclear Review provides a particular opportunity to do this.[3]

National Grid Company

Flotation of the National Grid Company (NGC) by the RECs is presently under active consideration. The form and timing of this is primarily a matter for its shareholders, the 12 RECs, and for the Government as holder of its 'golden share'. Nevertheless, there are regulatory aspects on which some comment may be appropriate.

Some might worry that a sale of NGC could have adverse implications for the continuity and security of electricity supply. However, the NGC has a statutory duty to develop and maintain an efficient, co-ordinated and economical system of electricity transmission. This duty is reinforced and amplified by the conditions of its licence. It will continue to have this duty, and its licence obligations, regardless of ownership. Other licensees, including public electricity suppliers and generators, have related duties and licence obligations, including the responsibility to comply with the Grid Code and the Distribution Code. These duties and obligations will also continue. I do not see any reason to fear there will be less continuity or security of supply if the RECs are no longer owners of NGC. There does not need to be common ownership of transmission and distribution in order to 'keep the lights on'. Indeed, before Vesting the transmission system was run by the CEGB, not the Area Boards.

Ownership of the NGC by the RECs has been acceptable as a transitional measure to facilitate privatisation, but whether this is appropriate for the future is another matter. The way in which the transmission grid is developed and operated is of significance for all parties in the industry including generators, regional companies, other suppliers including the Scottish companies, and other market participants. These parties have different interests and it is not appropriate that any one set of parties in the industry should be in a preferred position to influence the development and operation of the NGC's business.

---

3 *Editor's Note:* The conclusions of the Review were published as *The Prospects for Nuclear Power in the UK: Conclusions of the Government's Nuclear Review*, Cm. 2860, Department of Trade and Industry and the Scottish Office, London: HMSO, May 1995.

The prospects for competition between the NGC and the RECs (for example, in metering and settlements and provision of connections) would also be blunted by common ownership.

Continued ownership, control or ability to exert influence on the NGC by the RECs therefore seems increasingly inappropriate. Needless to say, ownership by any of the other major players in the industry would also be inappropriate. I have therefore indicated to the RECs my preference that they should sell their entire holdings in the NGC, preferably at flotation but if not within a specified but short period thereafter.

There will be benefits from the more efficient operation of the NGC, which I intend should be passed on to customers when the NGC's price control falls to be revised. I shall be starting this price control review shortly. As regards the increase in the value of the NGC since flotation, this may reflect various factors, including subsequent investment, a reduction in uncertainty about its prospects, and increased efficiency. It is not clear how far this increase should accrue to the RECs as a result of their transitional and 'hands off' ownership rôle. I therefore support the case for payments to customers as part of the NGC's flotation, to enable them to share in the financial benefits. It would also be advantageous to deal with this issue before the NGC's forthcoming price control review.

Pumped Storage Business

The question arises as to the future ownership of the NGC's Pumped Storage Business (PSB). One possibility would be to float it as part of the NGC, another to leave it with a combined REC Holding Company. I want to suggest that a third alternative would be preferable: to sell or dispose of PSB as a separate entity.

PSB consists of about 2,000 MW of plant at Dinorwic and Ffestiniog which has typically supplied about one-half of 1 per cent of the total output in England and Wales. However, its significance for competition is greater than these figures suggest. Its output is provided almost entirely at peak periods, and is the only significant supplier of non-baseload output apart from National Power and PowerGen. Last year it set SMP about 15 per cent of the time (with National Power and PowerGen setting it 47 and 37 per cent of the time respectively). PSB also supplies certain ancillary services in competition with other generators and has a particularly useful capacity for immediate response.

Although the NGC's initial ownership of PSB was an acceptable transitional measure during privatisation, I am not convinced this would be appropriate for the future. Directly or indirectly, PSB has the ability to influence SMP, constraint payments and other components of uplift. This could lead to increasing conflicts with the transmission business, especially after flotation and with new incentive arrangements for reducing uplift. It is important for the development of competition that transmission be clearly independent, and be seen to be independent, of interests in generation or supply.

In the light of experience over the last four years, and the licence obligations and other arrangements in place, continued NGC ownership of PSB no longer seems necessary on operational grounds. It will be necessary for the NGC (as transmission operator) to be able to call on the services of PSB and on terms which do not exploit any market power that PSB or NGC have, under whatever ownership. Arrangements for the contractual provision of ancillary services, and competitive bidding into the Pool, should help to ensure this. To the extent that further safeguards may be necessary, I would be prepared to consider appropriate licence modifications.

At the same time, it does not seem desirable for the RECs collectively to own PSB either. Ownership and control of PSB could enable it to be operated in the interests of its owners, with possible anti-competitive consequences. I am not convinced that 'self-denying ordinances' by RECs as owners would be either effective or consistent with management efficiency. Moreover, it does not seem to me desirable to provide an additional vehicle for the RECs to take a collective view about their interests. Nor, for obvious reasons, would it be desirable for the major generators to own PSB.

PSB is capable of operating as an independent company. I have therefore suggested to the RECs that they should dispose of their ownership of PSB, either at or by flotation or by means of a trade sale within a specified and short period of time.

The RECs and Competition

The final question I want to consider is what arrangements with respect to the RECs would be most conducive to more effective competition in the generation and supply of electricity, and to the full protection of customers' interests.

I start from two observations. *First*, it has been a central proposition in electricity privatisation that the transmission grid should as far as practicable be owned and operated independently of generation and supply. Admittedly, the NGC was given responsibility for PSB and the RECs formally owned the NGC, but these should be seen as essentially transitional arrangements to achieve privatisation in the time-frame available. There is now scope for ending these arrangements and establishing a proper separation of ownership.

Second, this separation of transmission ownership has been an acknowledged success. Admittedly, there have been complaints about the NGC, just as there have been about all other major licensees. But I am not aware of any complaints or deficiencies attributable to the separation of ownership. I believe it has made a major contribution to the development of competition to date. It is also a central element that other countries are increasingly adopting in reforming their own electricity industries.

In contrast, ownership of REC distribution networks was not separated from other REC activities. There were separate businesses for accounting purposes, but not separate ownership. This was understandable given the other significant restructuring and the uncertainties then associated with separate ownership of networks. But experience since Vesting has led to a wide range of concerns associated with the lack of separation. It seems to be widely believed that RECs are favoured by, and have often sought to exploit to their advantage, their positions as public electricity suppliers and owners and operators of the local distribution network. Concerns have included the relationship between distribution and the RECs' other activities such as ownership of generation and contracting with generators; supply into the non-franchise market, definition of the franchise/non-franchise boundary and associated conditions of supply; and retail and contracting activities. My investigations have not substantiated all the allegations that have been made, and where necessary I have taken appropriate action. Nevertheless, it seems that other REC businesses gain some advantage from common ownership of the distribution network and association with the rôle of the public electricity supplier.

There are other areas where ownership of the distribution network at the same time as engaging in generation, supply and other activities may cause difficulties in future. One is the establishing of satisfactory arrangements for full competition in 1998. Another is the possible development of RECs and others as integrated providers of utility services. I also have to say that setting a price control is complicated by the need to assess cost allocations between many businesses and the difficulty of distinguishing the past and prospective performance of one particular business within that of a whole group.

Some RECs have not engaged in generation, some are involved only minimally in second-tier supply, and some have withdrawn from retailing and other activities. This suggests that such activities are by no means essential to the efficient operation of the core distribution businesses. And if ownership and operation of the distribution business is material to the success of a REC's other activities, this in itself may be a cause for concern in the wider competitive context.

This issue is by no means straightforward. Amongst other things, satisfactory arrangements would need to be made for RECs to discharge their obligations as public electricity suppliers. Nevertheless, a variety of arrangements might be explored. These could include extending separate businesses to legal subsidiaries or a more physical separation of different activities. The successful precedent of the NGC's non-involvement in generation and supply as a condition of owning and operating the transmission network also suggests that this idea might be extended. There would therefore be merit in considering, amongst other possibilities, the separation of ownership and operation of REC local distribution networks from their activities in generation, supply and other businesses.

This may at first seem a novel idea. But it is no more than the application of the simple and established principle that clearer separation between monopoly networks and potentially competitive activities is more conducive to effective competition and full protection of customers.

Conclusions

There have been some significant achievements in the development of competition in generation. At Vesting, National Power and PowerGen together had 78 per cent of total output and capacity in England and Wales. Their output share is now below 60 per cent for the first time, and new entry continues to take place which will reduce it further. But their share of total capacity has fallen only half as fast, to 69 per cent. Their share of non-baseload output remains at about 95 per cent. Their sale or disposal of plant is thus an integral part of achieving a more competitive generating industry.

Nuclear Electric's share of total output is now over 23 per cent, and it already supplies more baseload output than PowerGen. It has market power in the Pool and contracts market. Competition would be enhanced by putting the Magnox plants under separate ownership and control, and transferring ownership of some AGR plants between Nuclear Electric and Scottish Nuclear.

The ownership of the NGC by the RECs has been acceptable as a transitional measure, but it is not appropriate that any one set of parties in the industry should be in a preferred position to influence the development and operation of the NGC's business. I have therefore indicated to the RECs my preference that they should sell their entire holdings in the NGC. I support the case for repayments to customers as part of NGC's flotation. I have also suggested that the RECs should dispose of their ownership of the Pumped Storage Business.

At Vesting, the transmission network was essentially separated from generation and supply. This arrangement has been a success. In contrast, REC distribution networks were not separated from supply, and generation has been added. Various concerns have been expressed, and other difficulties can be envisaged in the future. There would be merit in considering the separation of REC distribution networks from their activities in generation, supply and other businesses. Clearer separation between monopoly networks and potentially competitive activities is more conducive to effective competition and full protection of customers.

DISCUSSANT'S COMMENTS

Colin Robinson

Editorial Director, Institute of Economic Affairs;
Professor of Economics, University of Surrey

In THIS BRIEF COMMENT, my purpose is, *first*, to say a few general words about utility regulation in Britain, which is generally seen as in an unsatisfactory state; then, *second*, I shall turn to competition in electricity generation; *third*, I shall say something about how competition in generation can be promoted.

As I shall explain, in an industry such as electricity, privatised only four years ago, most of what has happened so far is a consequence of government decisions at the time of privatisation: only now are regulatory decisions beginning to have an influence. Most of the problems in utility markets are much more a consequence of ill-considered privatisation schemes than of poor regulation.

Privatisation and Regulation

Neo-classical economics has a tradition of seeking perfection. Many of my colleagues, imbued with that tradition, appear to be in search of perfect regulation. They analyse the imperfections of actual regulatory decisions and, urged on by some of the regulated companies, set out what the regulators do wrong. They tend to reach conclusions which depend on the assumption that there is a 'correct' way of regulating utilities which is common to all. So they usually conclude that we would be better off if all regulation was in the hands of one body or, at least, if there were some 'co-ordination'. That is the last thing we want. One day competition among regulators may produce 'best practice' regulation but since we do not know what that will be it should not be imposed now.

In searching for perfect regulation, they will be just as disappointed as in their earlier search for markets which either already were perfect or could be made so if only there existed perfect government. Perfect regulation cannot exist, any more than perfect markets or perfect governments, because knowledge is always and everywhere imperfect (if only because all knowledge relevant to decision-making is about the future). Indeed, it is as well to remind ourselves that regulation is such an unsatisfactory business – compared with the protection which competitive markets can offer consumers through the power of exit – that the best thing regulators can do is to pursue their pro-competition duties so assiduously that they rapidly shrink their offices towards zero.

The root of the problems of utility regulation in this country is the trail of unsatisfactory privatisation schemes left by the Thatcher governments. Generalising, but not I think unfairly, the emphasis was on political objectives such as revenue raising and widening share ownership. There was little effort to liberalise markets. What privatisation schemes achieved was to disengage government and to provide the necessary conditions for liberalised markets to appear. Markets which for years had suffered from state prohibition on entry became occupied instead by powerful private incumbents: in a phrase, entry to these markets moved from the impossible to the just very difficult.

In this scheme of things, the rôle of British utility regulators is far removed from traditional regulatory functions such as supervising natural monopolies and controlling their prices and standards of service. Their rôle is to supervise whole industries – only parts of which can reasonably be described as naturally monopolistic – and, using their pro-competition duties, to try to retrieve for consumers the benefits which better-considered privatisation schemes could have provided in the first place. They are, if you like, handmaidens of 'creative destruction'; they help accelerate a process which in the end will, in any event, destroy incumbent power.

As consumers, we need the regulators to stop the bulk of the efficiency gains from privatisation going for many years to shareholders and managers operating in not-very-rivalrous markets. Regrettably, in the early years, the principal benefits *have* mostly accrued to shareholders and managers. That is because government established régimes which encouraged productive efficiency gains, but provided no mechanism whereby those gains would be passed on to consumers. We should not blame regulators for the failings of government. But we should expect them, after the first few years, to take actions which channel the benefits of privatisation to consumers in terms of lower prices and better standards of service.

Electricity Privatisation and Regulation

What of electricity? Perhaps the fairest way to characterise the privatisation scheme is to say it was not bad as that for gas. It did split transmission from generation (despite dire warnings from the CEGB of the likely consequences of doing so), and it did split generation itself. But the division of the old CEGB's generation activities into only two companies is now widely recognised – even by those who did not realise it in advance – as a mistake. Regulation has suffered as a result.

When the Electricity Privatisation White Paper was published in February 1988, I see I wrote (in a somewhat better prediction than I usually manage) that the task of the electricity regulator would be 'extremely difficult if not downright impossible' given the Government's '...failure to establish an initial structure of generation which is clearly likely to stimulate competition'[1] and the RECs' ownership of the NGC. Not only did the Government fail to establish genuine competition in generation at that time; it failed to seize another opportunity in 1989 when it became clear that nuclear power could not be privatised; the restructuring which then became necessary, before privatisation, could have included a finer division of the fossil fuel generation sector.

The consequences for regulation have been extremely damaging. Electricity regulation has a wide scope, covering essentially the whole of a complex industry. Even though generation is naturally competitive and competition would be a far better protector of the interests of consumers than regulation can hope to be, the regulator has inevitably been drawn into supervising generation, partly in response to complaints from larger consumers. There have, I think, already been five weighty reports from Offer on the generation sector and it is clear that large amounts of valuable regulatory resources are being taken up in analysing behaviour in the Pool and making recommendations, most recently about capping prices and persuading the generators to agree to make reasonable endeavours to sell plant. Entry to the market has so far made little difference to the apparent ability of the duopolists to influence pool prices because they continue to have virtually all the marginal plant.

Price Trends

Prices are not the only concern of consumers, but I will say something about them before returning to competition in generation. Price statistics tell different stories according to which source one uses and whether they are expressed in nominal or real terms. I use DTI statistics, from *Energy Trends*, and express them in nominal terms which are most appropriate for my purpose.

There is no doubt that, so far, the results of electricity privatisation in terms of prices have been disappointing, even in the sector of the market where consumers have choice and despite considerable improvements in internal efficiency: the two major generators have, for example, cut their workforces by about two-thirds since privatisation and the RECs have made smaller cuts. Moreover, fuel input prices to generators have been substantially

---

[1] Colin Robinson, 'Liberalising the Energy Industries', *Proceedings of the Manchester Statistical Society*, March 1988, p.23.

reduced. In the first quarter of 1994, the major generators paid 28 per cent less for their coal than they did, on average, in 1988. The price of natural gas, which has only been used on any scale in power generation since early 1993, fell by 11 per cent between then and first quarter 1994. The price of fuel oil (now a minor fuel for electricity generation) has changed little on balance in the last five years.

To place movements in electricity prices in the context of changes in fuel prices in general, Figure 1 illustrates quarterly trends in coal, fuel oil, gas and electricity prices to industry (all expressed in thermal equivalent terms) since first quarter 1988. That period is taken as the starting point because the White Papers on electricity privatisation were published in February and March 1988: from then onwards, electricity prices began to adjust to the prospect of privatisation. The finishing point is first quarter 1994, just before the latest extension of the competitive market.

In essence, the Figure shows that, over this period, average coal prices to industry fell a little; gas prices fluctuated around a more-or-less constant level; and fuel oil prices did not change greatly on balance, though they

Fig. 1: Price of Fuels Purchased: GB Manufacturing Industry, 1988-94

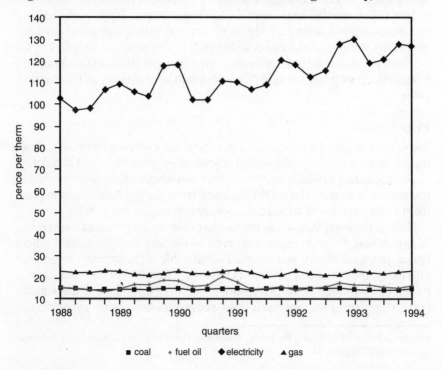

responded sharply to the Iraqi invasion of Kuwait in 1990. Despite the declining costs of labour and fuel inputs, electricity prices rose significantly – by about 24 per cent over the six years from first quarter 1988 to first quarter 1994, equivalent to an annual compound rate of just over 3¹/2 per cent.

Some specific factors in the electricity market help explain these big increases. One is the considerable price increases just before privatisation which were generally interpreted as government-inspired efforts to 'fatten up' the industry. Another is the loss of the old Qualifying Industrial Consumers' Scheme (QUICS), under which about 4 million tonnes of coal a year was provided to the CEGB by British Coal at around world prices: the benefits of the electricity deemed to be produced from this coal were passed on to about 400 large consumers under this scheme. Another factor is the gradual introduction of competition because of which only consumers of 1MW or over had a choice of supplier between vesting day and March 1994.

As Figure 2 shows, the companies which suffered most from electricity price increases are either very large consumers which lost their subsidies or

Fig. 2: Price of Electricity Purchased: GB Manufacturing Industry, 1989-94

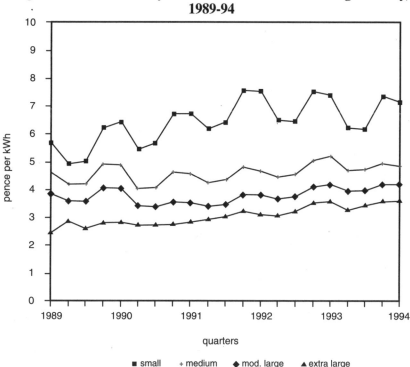

companies too small (less than 1MW) to have a choice of supplier before April 1994 and so outside the competitive market. According to DTI statistics, the first group – which includes large, energy-intensive consumers – has had a price increase of 46 per cent since first quarter 1989 (as far back as these statistics go) and the second group has had an increase of 26 per cent. These increases represent, respectively, annual average compound rates of almost 8 per cent and over $4^1/2$ per cent.

Moderately large and medium-size consumers – which have been in the competitive market from the beginning and had no subsidies to lose – have, as one would expect, fared better. They have had fairly small price increases of about 8 and 5 per cent respectively since first quarter 1989, compared with an increase in the producer price (output) index of about 20 per cent over the same period.

Outside the competitive market, residential consumers – who are the captives of their local RECs until 1998 – have also faced big increases in electricity prices in the last few years. Increases in domestic electricity prices have far outstripped increases in other domestic fuel prices since the late 1980s. Domestic electricity prices in first quarter 1994 were over 30 per cent higher than the average of 1988 whereas the price of gas (electricity's main competitor in homes) was only 14 per cent higher. Most of the increase in electricity prices took place between 1988 and 1991 since when prices have fallen slightly.

Competition in Generation

These price trends are not, of course, merely a consequence of what has happened in generation. But, since I do not have time to deal with the whole of the industry, let me return to competition in generation. It is, I think, inappropriate to blame National Power and PowerGen for their activities in the Pool: they are acting in what they perceive to be the interests of their shareholders. The source of the problem is the structure of generation. Structure is sometimes unimportant but I do not believe that to be so in this case where two companies (both offspring of a nationalised concern) are very significant players in an imposed and compulsory market (the Pool) which apparently lacks a characteristic which distinguishes genuine markets – the capacity to evolve in response to changing circumstances.

I am confident that entry will eventually eliminate the problem. But it is likely to take a long time and in the interim the regulatory office will continue to be diverted from its proper tasks of supervising use of the network of wires and avoiding exploitation of local monopolies by the RECs in the period up to 1998. Furthermore, National Power and PowerGen will be subject to intrusive regulation of a kind perhaps similar to that which eventually induced British Gas to refer itself to the MMC.

Stimulating Competition in Generation

To avoid such unfortunate outcomes, something out of the ordinary course of regulation is required. It might indeed be a reference of the generators to the MMC. But help might be at hand in the unlikely form of the Government's review of the nuclear industry. I am well aware that the Government would dearly wish not to have to review the nuclear industry: it would much prefer to sweep all matters nuclear under the carpet. However, as my nuclear review evidence suggested,[2] nuclear privatisation could be an effective means of restructuring generation.

Nuclear privatisation is desirable in itself. Nuclear needs to face a market test: the contest between it and other generation fuel sources should not be fought in terms of rival guesses about what costs will be, judged by civil servants, particularly since such guesses (and such judgements) have been so inaccurate in the past. Moreover, it is most unlikely that any new nuclear plant will be built while the industry is in state hands: the pressures on state finances are too great and the impact on privatised competitors would be too much. But, apart from its inherent desirability, nuclear privatisation could significantly enhance rivalry in generation. I would suggest the following:

- Privatise Nuclear Electric and Scottish Nuclear (Magnox apart; this should be contracted out to minimise operating costs or franchised as a separate activity) as companies with generation as their main business, able to diversify, sell their electricity where they choose and generally enjoy commercial freedom.

- Allocate some of Nuclear Electric's plant to Scottish Nuclear so that the companies are more equal in size.

- Remove all state support for nuclear power and all geographical market-sharing arrangements so there is an 'internal market' in electricity throughout Britain (and before long throughout the United Kingdom).

---

2 Colin Robinson, *Privatising Nuclear Power: evidence for the review of future prospects for nuclear power*, Surrey Energy Economics Discussion Paper No.79, Guildford: University of Surrey, November 1994.

There would then be two formidable new competitors for National Power and PowerGen, with sites connected to the grid and knowledge of how the electricity market functions, able to compete in the Pool and throughout the contract market in Britain. The likely result would be both lower prices and contract terms better tailored to individual requirements.

The Government has a record of missing opportunities to enhance competition in generation so I am not confident it will seize this one. If it does not, a reference to the MMC seems to me the most likely next step.

8

REGULATION: SPECIAL VERSUS GENERAL

Sir Bryan Carsberg
Office of Fair Trading

Introduction

WHEN MICHAEL BEESLEY ASKED ME to give this lecture, and suggested the title 'Regulation: Special Versus General', I imagine he had in mind that the title would give me plenty of freedom to discuss a range of issues of topical importance. I should like to interpret it in that way. I will comment on the choice between special and general regulators but I do not think that this is the most important issue in modern regulation and I do think that it is inter-related with a number of other issues. I therefore intend to cast my paper rather more generally, and perhaps 'The Structure of Regulation' might be more descriptive of my intention.

When Graeme Odgers began this series of lectures, seven weeks ago, he opened with a quotation from Richard Whish, stating that UK competition law was a 'bizarre and complex structure'.[1] The intervening lectures have delved into a number of more specific issues but I want to bring you full circle back to the question of the overall structure. Complex it is! Bizarre? I am less certain, but it is perhaps untidy, evidently something which has grown up piecemeal, with extra bits patched on to deal with new problems as they have arisen. It has the appearance of being, as it is, a rather early model judged against the versions of many countries with which we work in the European Union or the OECD.

In the days, now many years passed, when I used to have time for such things, I took an enthusiastic interest in cosmology and I used to enjoy drawing on cosmological analogies. Perhaps the appropriate one for our competition law is the Ptolemaic system to describe the movements of the planets. The Greeks of the time were burdened by the belief that the Earth must be the centre of the Universe and that the planets must therefore move in circles around it. As observations improved, the initial

---

[1] R. Whish, *Competition Law, op.cit.,* p.730 (see above, page 1, note 1).

assumptions were discredited and the inconsistency was solved for a time by assuming that planets moved in circles which were centred on, and moving round, other circles. Over time, circles were added to circles, and yet more circles, until, if my memory serves me correctly, some 40 or 50 circles were involved. Only in the Middle Ages, with the work of Copernicus and Kepler, was this unwieldy edifice swept away and replaced by the elegant simplicity of the ellipse. Is the grafting of new laws dealing with competition on to old laws rather like the development of the Ptolemaic system? Are we now awaiting the Copernican revolution of competition law? We all will have our views on this although, on reflection, I am not quite sure that the analogy with movement in circles and ellipses quite catches the spirit of directness and progress that I would favour!

The Regulatory Scene

Financial Services

Let us come back to Earth and consider some of the actual regulatory situations facing some of our businesses. Financial Services is not a bad place to start. Here, the first tier of regulation comprises the self-regulatory organisations, bodies like the Personal Investment Authority and several others, including professional bodies such as the accountancy bodies and the Law Society. These bodies make rules about a number of matters, including retail selling practices, which have effects on competition. They operate under the auspices of the Securities and Investments Board. I have the duty of keeping their rules under review and reporting to the Chancellor of the Exchequer on any aspects of them which appear to me to be significantly anti-competitive. The Chancellor has the power to order a change in the rules although he is not bound to accept my opinion on these matters. In addition, parts of the industry are subject to separate prudential regulation, for example, the insurance industry by the Department of Trade and Industry and banking by the Bank of England. There are also codes of practice of some industry associations which the firms have agreed to observe.

The Media

Another interesting example of complexity in regulation concerns the media. The regulation of independent television companies, including off-air broadcasting and cable television companies, in accordance with the Broadcasting Act 1990, is undertaken by the Independent Television Commission. This body has responsibility particularly for programming; also it has a duty to promote competition. Independent radio is regulated by the Radio Authority. Some of the broadcasters, notably cable television companies, operate telecommunications systems for the distribution of their programmes. They are regulated by OFTEL. Radio spectrum is allocated and regulated in use by the Radiocommunications Agency, an Executive Agency which reports to the Department of Trade and Industry. The BBC does not come under the Independent Television Commission or the Radio Authority and, in a sense, is its own regulator. I have some specific responsibilities in relation to these matters. Under the Broadcasting Act, I have powers to require changes in the networking arrangements of the independent television companies, on competition grounds, subject to appeal to the Monopolies and Mergers Commission. I also have to monitor the BBC's performance against the goal of commissioning 25 per cent of 'qualifying programmes' from independent producers. And the general competition law is applicable to these industries.

The Utilities

Next we might note the position of the utilities. As they have been privatised, most of the utilities have been brought under specialised regulatory régimes, administered by specialised regulators. The regulatory bodies are constitutionally similar to the Office of Fair Trading, with statutory responsibility in the hands of a Director General. All are non-ministerial government departments. All have some duty of promoting or maintaining competition and some functions under the general competition law jointly with me. The effect is that the Directors General of the specialist regulatory bodies have overlapping functions with mine, as regards promoting competition, although often they have the alternative of taking pro-competitive action under their licensing arrangements or other specialist regulatory instruments. Some functions in these industries are carried out by the appropriate Secretary of State, for example, the licensing of public telecommunications operators. Mergers involving utilities fall under my functions in that it is for me to advise the Secretary of State on action, even though, of course, I would fully consult the specialist regulator.

The Offices of the specialist regulators are OFTEL, OFGAS, OFWAT and OFFER, and the Office of the Rail Regulator. No doubt, I should add the Civil Aviation Authority with regard to airports and the Electricity Regulator for Northern Ireland. Water is still state-owned in Scotland and the Secretary of State has functions there. And I almost forgot OFLOT.[2]

---

[2] The body regulating the National Lottery.

The bus industry provides the major example of privatisation for which no specialist regulatory régime was established but for which reliance on the general competition law was preferred. And it is, to put it gently, debatable as to whether that was the best course.

Fitting the OFT into the Jigsaw

How does the Office of Fair Trading fit into the pattern? The essentials will be well-known to people by now. My mainstream functions come under the Fair Trading Act 1973. This creates the two important categories of monopoly investigations: the simple monopoly, where one firm has a market share of 25 per cent or more, and the complex monopoly where firms together have 25 per cent or more and carry on their businesses in ways which restrict, prevent or distort competition. My rôle is essentially to conduct a preliminary investigation to establish whether or not a complex or simple monopoly seems to exist and, of course, whether there is some reason to think that it might be regarded as operating against the public interest. If these conditions are met, I may make a monopoly reference to the MMC. It investigates and reports its assessment of the public interest to the Secretary of State for Trade and Industry who decides on action. For mergers, the process is similar but involves an extra step. I investigate and advise the Secretary of State on whether or not the merger may operate against the public interest; the Secretary of State decides whether or not to refer to the MMC; if a reference is made the MMC reports back to the Secretary of State; and if the MMC finds the merger to operate or to be *likely* to operate against the public interest, further action is at the discretion of the Secretary of State.

I have functions under numerous other Acts, and I have mentioned some of them already. But I will develop the picture sufficiently for present purposes if I add a word or two about my functions under the Restrictive Trade Practices legislation. This deals with the registration of agreements under which two or more parties accept restrictions on their behaviour. If an agreement qualifies for registration, I put it on a public register and consider whether or not it should be referred to the Restrictive Practices Court to seek a judgment on whether or not the agreement is acceptable in the public interest. If I wish not to take the agreement to Court, I must seek permission from the Secretary of State not to do so. Subject to that, further decisions about whether any part of the agreement should be struck down are in the hands of the Court.

I should also mention that almost any British business may be affected by the competition provisions of the Treaty of Rome.

I have, of course, been selective in the types of regulation I have mentioned. I could have mentioned many others, even for the industries I have covered: for example, regulation under company law, health and safety regulation, environmental matters, and, indeed, rather closer to the examples I have mentioned, the many statutory powers exercised by local authority Trading Standards Officers. Had I brought in other industries, I would have shown some extra twists and turns in the labyrinth. However, I have perhaps gone far enough with my description to establish a basis for discussion of the main approaches. I have mentioned examples of self-regulatory organisations, both voluntary and within a statutory framework, and examples of regulation by bodies external to the industry concerned. I have mentioned examples of regulation by individuals, the Directors General, and by Commissions, Boards or Committees. I have mentioned industry-specific regulators as well as regulators with authority across the whole of the private sector of the economy. I have mentioned regulation by private sector bodies, by quangos, and by bodies in the public sector, both public officials acting independently of government ministers and government ministers acting directly.

Future Development of Competition Policy Regulation

I will give my thoughts on the merits of these approaches later. However, before doing so, I will briefly comment on my hopes for the future development of regulation under competition policy. First, a word about process. Much recent controversy about regulation has been focussed on the accusation that regulators have too much power and that they sometimes use it arbitrarily without giving enough attention to what our US friends would call 'due process'. I have always thought that the critics who voiced these concerns exaggerated the problems which had actually arisen. In general, I think that the regulators have consulted widely and effectively and have usually, though not invariably, given good and helpful explanations of their decisions. I also think that, in practice, the regulated businesses have had plenty of opportunity to put forward their case. They have not had all that they wanted: nor should they have done. But the shortfalls have not arisen significantly because of lack of due process.

Nevertheless, it is very important to foster confidence in regulation both by the general public and the regulated businesses which must have the confidence to invest. Everything possible should be done to put process beyond criticism. Wide-ranging consultation should be undertaken wherever possible, with a good deal of openness. (I have adopted the practice at OFT of holding public hearings on policy questions such as the extent of desirable consumer credit regulation and have found them to work extremely well.) The regulated business should have clear

127

knowledge of the issues, so that it has every opportunity to put its point of view fully and forcefully, and it should have reasonable, although not unlimited, time for doing so. Regulators should give broad explanations of their decisions – enough to be helpful for the regulated business in its strategic planning. I also think that some kind of appeal mechanism is desirable, at least on major issues and where the initial decision is in the hands of an individual. Most of this can be attained within the present framework. All the regulators are conscious of the need for good process and, I think, would agree with much of what I have said. Procedures have been tightened up recently and happily one does not hear much complaint on the subject nowadays.

However, not everything I have suggested is attainable within the existing framework of law. For example, an appeal process is sometimes attainable in effect only if the regulated business forces an issue to the MMC, as we have seen recently in a few of the price control cases for water and electricity. In some other cases, an appeal mechanism could perhaps be contrived, for example, by taking advantage of overlapping functions. However, this would not be possible for all cases and regulators are anyway properly unhappy about contrivance. A change in the law would be needed to achieve a more satisfactory situation overall.

Views about process may affect choice of regulatory structure. For example, it would be difficult for government ministers to participate personally in a due process – as would be desirable if they were the decision-maker – except perhaps occasionally in special situations. On the other hand, involvement of the Courts automatically calls up use of a particular kind of due process, although it also puts the process heavily in the hands of lawyers who may not be the best people to judge the general public interest in competition policy cases.

Regulatory Institutions and the Law

I next want to mention some of my ambitions for changes to the law because, in thinking about the institutional structures one wishes to have in place, it is important to take account of how the law may be in future and not just how it is today. As I have been heard to say before, my foremost ambition for changes to competition law relates to the law on restrictive trade practices. The present position under this part of our law is that nothing is initially prohibited. Prohibitions can occur only after investigation and formal action by one or more authorities. I think this approach is weak. Some might argue that it has the merit of avoiding the danger of ill-defined jeopardy for the businesses concerned. However, any such benefit is obtained at the expense of greater delay and uncertainty for others, who are generally the weaker parties. Furthermore, certain kinds of behaviour are now widely agreed to be competition offences; they can be defined and prohibited without undue difficultly. It would be a step forward to adopt such a prohibition approach, with stiff penalties for breaches of the law. The possibility that even behaviour covered by these offences can sometimes be judged in the public interest can be allowed for by a procedure to obtain exemptions. This is the approach adopted in the Treaty of Rome and it is the approach which the Government committed itself to adopt in a 1989 White Paper.

The prohibition approach would require some institutional changes. Questions would arise as to who would levy fines, who would prosecute cases and what the appeal mechanism would be. One possibility is that my Office would become more like a prosecutor, perhaps with limited ability to impose fines in the first instance, subject to appeal to a tribunal that might reside in the MMC.

Refusal to Supply

The Government's commitment to move towards a prohibition system relates to restrictive agreements. There are other kinds of anti-competitive behaviour which do not involve agreements – at least not agreements that can be identified – and yet may be able to be defined with reasonable precision. I have in mind such things as predatory pricing and refusal to supply, instances of what may be an abuse of a dominant position. I will focus briefly on refusal to supply, a matter of concern to me in a number of industries.

I recognise that refusal to supply is often well justified. I would also accept that many small and medium-sized businesses should simply be allowed to please themselves about with whom they deal. However, one comes across some industries with oligopolistic structures where refusal to supply appears to be systematic and perhaps directed towards certain kinds of retailers – that is, those who are known to be discounters. Presumably this is not a way of making excess profits for the manufacturers unless competition is limited at that level. It does seem likely to be part of a club-like arrangement and likely to reduce consumer choice and inhibit the development of new kinds of retailing. It also seems likely to increase the frictions in competitive systems such that the forces of competition work less well in general than they otherwise would – and, at best, competition is likely to work fairly imperfectly in most industries.

I am, therefore, moving towards the view that I would like to see prohibition of certain kinds of behaviour not covered by agreements, such as predatory pricing and refusal to supply, with exemptions for particular circumstances such as poor creditworthiness and lack of technical competence where it is relevant, and with reasonably generous exemptions based on size or market share of the firm, and also with provision for exemption on prior application in the public interest. More work will have to be done to establish the feasibility of these proposals but I believe they are worth considering.

Self- or External Regulation?

I now turn to make a few more comments on the choices of regulatory structure. First, a short comment on self-regulation as compared to external regulation. Regulators, of course, will accept any proper source of help available in achieving their objectives. Frequently, I find that self-regulation (for example, in the form of codes of practices applied by trade associations) can produce significant improvements for customers. This is most visible in improving the assurance with which a certain quality of service is delivered, but it can have a useful impact on matters such as transparency of terms and conditions. However, self-regulation relies on a reasonable identity of interest between the industry and the regulator or on back-up statutory powers which can be expected to be used effectively. These conditions are often lacking. Self-regulation is evidently unfitted to deal with the broad problems of competition law.

The next choice perhaps is industry-specific regulation versus general regulation. Debates on this choice are usually about whether we should have formed so many different regulatory bodies, particularly for the utilities but also for some of the other fields I have mentioned. When the second of the modern utility regulatory régimes was being established (that for gas), the issue was widely discussed. I expressed the view that it might be better to have separate bodies for telecoms and gas. I saw some advantage in variety, especially since regulation was primarily in the hands of individuals. Utility regulation of this type was a new experience for the UK and indeed was being carried out in circumstances unique in the world. No doubt much learning would be needed. There would be some false trails. A variety of regulators is perhaps best calculated to ensure that the learning process is as effective as possible. I do not think that the argument that economies could be achieved in a consolidated regulatory body has much force. There are good channels of communication among the regulatory bodies and such learning from experience as is feasible can take place well under present arrangements. I do think it was helpful to have the highly concentrated focus of specialised regulatory bodies in the early years, when there was emphasis on the need for the regulator to move the industry actively in promoting competition, and to contribute in various ways to the transition to the private sector. However, I wonder whether the process was taken too far. I had thought that gas and electricity might have been combined because of the overlapping natures of the markets. And railways and buses?

Regulatory Specialisation

I have at least a slight preference, on balance, for some degree of specialisation in regulation, although I would add that I doubt whether it matters very much. If there had been a single regulatory body it would have needed divisions, with much the same sort of activity as the present separate regulators, and the heads of the divisions would have had a vital rôle. I think this would have worked a little less well, if only because of the desirability of involvement by the decision-maker, but perhaps also because of the difficulty of recruiting people of sufficient ability at a level below that of head of department.

Of course, the view that things have been quite well done in the initial period is not the same as the view that they should remain that way once we get to a more mature situation. It is not too difficult to justify specialised régimes when a period of transition is in process, but it may be rather harder to do so when an industry reaches maturity. It is at least hard to justify the application of a different competition policy in aspects of industries like telecommunications or perhaps gas supply when they have become reasonably competitive. We cannot yet be sure about the extent to which a position of some stability will be reached and the extent to which continuing effort will be needed to maintain some level of competition. Continuing effort actively to maintain competition may be needed, may be justifiable and may warrant the continuation of special regulatory arrangements.

Choice of Regulator the Key? Directors General *v*. Commission

However, the key to the maintenance of separate specialist regulatory bodies may also lie in the choice between Director General as regulator and Commission as regulator. To this I now turn. I am not an impartial observer on this subject. However, I do not think that regulation by Director General has worked out at all badly. A great deal of complaining by the regulated companies about the so-called cult of personality, associated with regulation by Director General, has taken place and been linked with complaints about arbitrary decisions, high-handed behaviour and imperfections in due process. No doubt to some extent these complaints were not so much a sign of a real feeling of having been unfairly treated, as the result of a wish to show shareholders and colleagues that everything possible was being done to press for favourable treatment. No doubt, also, there was an element of inevitability about the regulatees' feeling sincerely that there was an element of hardship in decisions.

An advantage of regulation by Director General, I think, has been the possibility it creates of relatively speedy and firm decision-making on a consistent track. I realise that this comment on consistency contradicts some of the complaints. But Commissions often make compromises because they wish to get a reasonable measure of agreement among members and the compromises may lack consistency because a rather different balance is struck from time to time. When I was Director General of Telecommunications, I used to make a strong point in my speeches of emphasising the importance I attached to competition, indicating that I would go to all reasonable lengths to secure an environment which was favourable to competition. I thought it was important to give this signal to people who might be potential competitors in telecoms markets. I think, today, that my doing so had a strong and beneficial effect on the market. However, I well remember one occasion when my speech was heard by the Chairman of the US Federal Communications Commission. He expressed surprise at the firm line I had taken, saying that he would not be able to do this as part of achieving his objectives because he had to think about whether the other Commissioners would agree, and they might well not do so or resent being taken for granted. He said this from the perspective of someone who agreed with my broad policies.

Of course, another Director General might have taken a different line. He or she might have said that, although the law called for the promotion of competition, one could not expect very much actually to be possible. The law allows wide discretion and the procedures for selecting Directors General provide scant safeguard. Regulation by Director General may be a risky business. Because of the risk, I am inclined to think that the time will come when pressure builds up to move from regulation by Director General to regulation by Commission. Although I would not advocate this, it will matter much less in the future than it would have done immediately after privatisation, and I suspect that it can be made to work reasonably well. The balance of argument about the need for specialised regulatory bodies may also change then.

Independent or Government Regulation?

The last contrast on which I wish to comment is that between regulators who are independent of the Government and regulation by government ministers. The Governments of the 1980s made the bold decision that regulation of the privatised utilities should be largely independent of ministers, and this brought substantial benefits and will do so for years to come. No doubt, they were persuaded particularly by the thought that potential shareholders would be sceptical about the merits of investment if government continued to have too strong a rôle because of the view that government influence in the past, when the industries were nationalised, had often been commercially and economically damaging. A clean break was needed. This apart, however, there are strong grounds for believing that ministerial involvement in the details of regulation is inappropriate. Ministers do not have the time to immerse themselves in the subject to the extent that is desirable for decisions of this kind. They may be too vulnerable to the political fashions and pressures of the time to pursue a consistent policy and political objectives may anyway produce results which are different from the needs of economic regulation. It is difficult, as a practical matter, for ministers to participate in due process and their involvement may therefore result in a low score for process. Furthermore, increasingly, competition policy and related matters are the focus of efforts at international harmonisation because competition takes place at a transnational level and competition policy requires to be regarded as fair at that level. Political involvement is likely to work against this aim. It is out of step with the trend of the times.

I hasten to add that in putting forward this argument I make no criticism of the behaviour of current ministers and I make no prediction about what will happen under ministers in the near future. I simply think that, even if things have worked relatively well up to now, the time will come in the future when ministerial involvement will serve us poorly. The Government would do a great service to the future if it were to grasp the nettle now of making revisions to the rôle of ministers. In a nutshell, I simply do not think that it makes sense for government ministers to be judging what to do about predatory pricing, refusal to supply or matters covered by restrictive agreements.

Of course, if we move to a prohibition system for much of competition policy, ministerial involvement would naturally fall away. The proper rôle of ministers is to set the framework of law within which these matters are settled and perhaps to deal with issues involving major restructuring of industries. For example, ministerial involvement is probably inevitable in decisions such as those relating to the tied estate of the brewing industry.

Concluding Remarks

I will conclude with just two further comments. First, I recognise that revision of a regulatory régime can be risky. The results may be unexpected and the political processes involved in revision may produce sub-optimal results. Things are not working badly at present; indeed, in many respects, they are working well. However, if I am right in thinking that pressure is building up to the point some review will become inevitable, then I would be inclined to take the risk and look for a broad re-evaluation.

My second point concerns variability of the regulatory régime. I have already emphasised the desirability of having a well-defined régime and I have suggested that this could be done better than it is. It is also important, I think, for there to be a consistent regulatory régime without too many special provisions – that is, without too many Ptolemaic circles. At present we have considerable variety of régime carried in numerous different statutes. The variety imposes a considerable cost on business which must deal with all the different approaches. Perhaps the variety also makes people lose sight of just how great the total cost is. There is also the variance between the British approach and the European approach which I have hardly mentioned in this paper because of space limitations. Perhaps the time cannot now long be postponed for reviewing the system and producing greater consistency. Perhaps we are ready for our Copernican revolution.

DISCUSSANT'S COMMENTS

Sir Christopher Foster
Coopers & Lybrand

As ONE HAS COME TO EXPECT, Sir Bryan Carsberg has ranged over a number of topics in his paper and has been both direct and interesting in what he has said. Necessarily, my remarks must be selective. Thus though sorely tempted, I will not follow him in his remarks on the sheer complexity of the various regulatory arrangements that exist in Britain or in his questioning whether there is any longer any rationale or theory which justifies or even explains their diversity, let alone the interaction of our institutions with those in Europe or, for that matter, the United States as it reaches out across the world.

There are three reasons why I am not going to add to what he has said about procedures. *First*, I have myself written about these matters at some length elsewhere.[1] *Second*, I agree entirely with what he has said. *Third*, we have also recently had Ian Byatt's paper to this forum on 'The Importance of Process in Economic Regulation', in which he describes his own procedures.[2]

My own conclusion is that I do not believe the regulators have been procedurally inadequate. Their procedures are in general as defensible as Ian Byatt's are, but I do believe it would have been sensible if everyone had been as painstaking and careful, not so much for the sake of natural justice, for I know of no evidence that has been impugned, but for the wider acceptability, preservation and development of the system.

Prohibitions and Fines

I will make some brief remarks on prohibitions and fines. I do not disagree with Bryan Carsberg on either scope or need. One must take care to avoid increasing regulators' powers unless one can reasonably argue their necessity. However, the absence of powers to prohibit can have results

---

[1] C.D. Foster, *Privatisation, Public Ownership and the Regulation of Natural Monopoly*, Oxford: Blackwell, 1992, Ch.8, and two papers published by the Centre for Regulated Industries: 'Natural Monopoly – Is Change Required?', 1994, and 'Natural Justice and the Process of Natural Monopoly Regulation of Natural Justice', forthcoming, 1995.

[2] See above, Chapter 2: 'Water: The Periodic Review Process', pp.21-30.

which may be almost scandalous in failing to allow effective action. One only has to look at the bus industry to see how companies may be destroyed before it is possible for the existing machinery to work.

More generally, the presumption behind the existing law was that companies would respect findings; but the number of players subject to regulation has generally increased, even in the natural monopoly areas, and there are sometimes complex and shifting patterns of ownership. Therefore tougher incentives to deter misbehaviour are probably needed. However, I do believe that if there are to be prohibitions and fines, the courts will have to be brought in – not on issues which, I agree with Bryan Carsberg, should be or become the preserve of the natural monopoly regulators, that is, the DGFT and the MMC, nor only on matters normally covered by judicial review, but also to check that the penalties are not disproportionate to the offence. I doubt if regulators could get away with levying substantial fines without such protection. It follows also that there must always be a right of appeal on merits, preferably to the MMC, if fines are to be levied.

I come to my first point of slight disagreement: specialist versus generalist regulation. Even here I agree with him over much: for example, that the importance of this issue can be exaggerated and that there are good channels of communication between regulators. I would go further and point to the example of the formal standing arrangements which Ian Byatt has helped develop, to deal with persistent issues that lie at the interfaces between various economic regulators and between them and other regulators. More such arrangements will be needed, I suspect, between energy regulators and between the rail regulator and OFT over buses.

Information Asymmetry: A Lasting Problem

There are two reasons why I am rather more than marginally against going further by combining some of our present regulators in two, let alone into a single college. The *first* is that I see information asymmetry as a lasting problem. Regulators need to know the economics and the technology of the industry. I believe one lesson for the future from recent price reviews is that regulators would be better advised to rely on technical knowledge of best practice in the rest of the world, and of how it might be adopted and adapted to our own circumstances, than to rely overmuch on yardstick competition. In any case, effective regulation requires specialised knowledge which must be continuously developed. Ultimately, I believe that the success of natural monopoly regulation will depend more on detailed knowledge of the regulated industry at home and abroad than on either economic theory or regulatory consistency. Regulators also need to know the players in the industry well: their number is ever-increasing.

The difference between specialist and generalist regulators has to be based, if it is rational, on a difference between industries where one has to expect regulation to be continuous – even though its focus may change – and industries which are competitive enough for it to be occasional. I think the time has come to recognise that the need for regulation will not disappear so long as there remains major natural monopoly to which ensuring equal access continues to be an issue.

No Secrecy but Openness: References to MMC

The *second* reason against merging regulators is even more important. I do not believe that differences in the application of competition should be ironed out behind closed doors in a college of regulators but openly through references to the MMC and, possibly also as I have suggested, through retrospective Section 78 reviews by the MMC,[3] but influenced also by detailed academic research into decisions. In saying this, I accept that the MMC may need to take steps to ensure its own greater consistency.

Pressure may well build up to replace individual regulators by commissions. That would be a pity for the reasons Bryan Carsberg has given and for other reasons I have given elsewhere. Though not of the first importance, such amalgamation would be a failure of the system because a working appeal system is a better and more accountable method of achieving consistency. Bryan Carsberg has suggested that the need to achieve consensus on a commission may prevent clarity in expressing its decisions. There is American evidence to suggest that it may also compromise and muddy decision-making in a weakly chaired commission; or not affect the outcome where the chairman is strong. It is not accidental that appeal court judges generally, as I understand it, either concur with another's opinion or express their own.

The Rôle of Ministers

Now I turn to what is perhaps the most important issue of all which Sir Bryan Carsberg has raised: the rôle of ministers. *First*, someone ought to trace through and try to rationalise the many different ways in which ministers enter into the various parts of our regulatory systems. There has been such proliferation of points and kinds of entry provided for them that I wonder if it is any longer possible to rationalise them with any

---

3 Provided for in Section 78 of the Fair Trading Act.

coherence; but I suspect there are two leading and long-standing notions here that underly many of the provisions.

The first is the right of ministers to state policy. John Swift pointed out in his paper how his legislation was special in that it provided for ministers to give him guidelines;[4] and in the other natural monopoly legislation there is provision for the Secretary of State to suggest priorities to the regulator. However, I believe I am right in stating that ministers really do not have to have special powers to do either of these. There were many ministerial White Papers and other policy statements in the old days on such matters as Energy Policy, Aviation Policy, Investment and Pricing criteria, and so on; but they did not have the force of law. They were guidelines to the boards of nationalised industries which could not and in practice did not prejudice their independence.

There would be considerable advantage in there being government policy statements on similar issues in future, such as the following: given the exhaustibility of various fuel sources and the likely development of environmental policy, what weight regulators might give, consistent with the law and their duties, to the preservation of means of supplying energy which will be needed much more in, say, 50 years time than now. Or to help the Rail Regulator decide what weight to give to changes in road taxation and pricing because of the congestion and environmental pollution which may be likely to affect the relative cost and therefore use of transport modes. Just as much as the old nationalised industry White Papers, they cannot be more than guidelines, given the statutory independence of the regulators, which is necessary to them in their quasi-judicial rôles.

Tradition of Quasi-Judicial Ministerial Casework

However, there are other long-standing rôles of ministers which are themselves quasi-judicial. They come from the same tradition as that which uses JPs rather than trained lawyers in magistrates' courts: from the belief that experienced laymen, indeed often because they have acute political antennae, can make certain decisions better (as well as more quickly and cheaply) than lawyers can. Not many decades ago in most government departments, such casework occupied a substantial part of ministerial time. In many they remain important, and I would suppose ministerial decisions on competition policy are among them.

In these rôles, ministers in general had to go through various procedures to demonstrate their fairness and open-mindedness, relying substantially

---

4 See Chapter 5: 'Regulatory Relationships Between Key Players in the Restructured Rail Industry', above, pp.65-79.

on impartial civil service briefing. Judicial review decided, for example, that they could not give their view on what the outcome of a planning decision should be before all parties have put their case. Their decisions would be expected to reflect their stated policies, presuming that these are lawful. While other political considerations may be at work, there is a presumption that such decisions will be seen as disinterested and fair-minded. There are also issues of appropriateness. One would not expect a Home Secretary to grant a pardon because a convicted criminal was vital to his firm, however important that firm was to the economy; or a planning decision to be decided because the beneficiary was a political supporter.

Promotion of Competition and the 'National Interest'

In an area like competition policy, we must expect changes in policy to lead to changes in interpretation; but such a change as has taken place recently perhaps requires more explanation than it has yet had. Under Peter Lilley, the promotion of competition seemed to be the overriding policy objective and because of it many mergers and acquisitions were referred to the MMC. Indeed, the competition staff was greatly increased at the DTI to ensure the effectiveness of this policy.

Michael Heseltine, on assuming office, indicated that questions of national interest would have greater weight with him, as indeed they might seem to have had. However, is one right to wonder, from the decisions he has made, whether we have had any indication of the circumstances in which he would now use his discretion to refer a merger or acquisition to the MMC? Or to put one's worry another way: if competition is to have any weight at all in his decisions, what balance is he trying to strike between that and his interpretation of the national interest? Much wasted effort might be avoided by greater clarity in these matters.

There is also an issue here of due process, as Bryan Carsberg has indicated. Perhaps the time has come to question whether ministers should, for example, any longer have a rôle in the clearance of restrictive agreements, or in the vetoing of monopoly references to the MMC. It is very hard to think of a good reason for this rôle, unless one believes regulators' recommendations might be vexatious or frivolous. Moreover, is one wrong to think that perhaps what is required is that, once the MMC has reported, ministers in their quasi-judicial capacities should, like regulators, give clear and principled reasons for their decisions, especially when these depart from MMC findings? They already have to do so in other similar areas.

ECONOMIC AFFAIRS

The journal of the IEA
Spring 1995
Financial Regulation issue
(edited by Professor Harold Rose)

Main Articles

Harold Rose	Introduction
George Benston	'The Sins of Banking Regulation in the USA'
David Llewellyn	'Regulation of Retail Investment Services'
Maureen O'Hara	'Derivatives: What's Needed to Protect the Financial Markets?'
Donald Brash	'Banking Supervision: New Zealand Adopts a New Approach'
Harold Rose	'Financial Regulation - The Underlying Issues'
Jim Stretton	'Regulating Life Assurance: Objectives and Machinery'

Individual issue £2.50

Annual subscriptions:

UK & Europe: £15.00 (Institution); £10.00 (Individual);
Rest of the World: £20.00/$35.00 (Surface); £30.00/$50.00 (Air)

Please apply to:

The Institute of Economic Affairs
2 Lord North Street, Westminster
London SW1P 3LB
Telephone: 0171-799 3745   Fax: 0171-799 2137

The Centralisation of Western Europe
ROLAND VAUBEL

1. Classical liberals dislike centralisation; they prefer decentralised decision-making because it takes into account individual preferences and permits competition among governments.

2. In Europe, centralisation (political integration) stifles competition and ignores differences in preferences.

3. Many so-called 'competitive distortions' are not distortions at all: they reflect differences in preferences and factor endowments.

4. Uniform European regulations – for example, to harmonise social regulations, taxes and environmental standards – create distortions.

5. The European Union has taken over functions which, 'under an efficient division of labour, belong to the member-states, lower levels of government or individual citizens'.

6. Centralisation in the Union results not from the quest for economic efficiency but from a flawed political structure within which bureaucrats, politicians and judges pursue their own interests and pressure groups have great influence.

7. The European Commission is a bureaucracy and yet part of the legislative process; the European Parliament reinforces the Commission's centralising tendencies; the European Court of Justice is an 'engine' of integration; the Council of Ministers may act as a 'European cartel of politicians'.

8. Centralising measures are hard to reverse because of a ratchet effect (recognised in the *acquis communautaire* doctrine).

9. National parliaments should control Union legislation, there should be referenda on major issues, separate machinery from the Court of Justice is required to determine subsidiarity issues, and the Commission should no longer be the 'legislative agenda setter'.

10. The legitimacy of policy centralisation can derive only from democracy – which is what the Union lacks. Institutional and procedural reform is the only effective cure.

ISBN 0-255 36343-5

Hobart Paper 127

£8.60
incl. p&p

The Institute of Economic Affairs
2 Lord North Street, Westminster
London SW1P 3LB
Telephone: 0171 799 3745
Fax: 0171 799 2137